PLENTY

PLENTY

CORINNE LEE

PENGUIN POETS

PENGUIN BOOKS

An imprint of Penguin Random House LLC
375 Hudson Street
New York, New York 10014
penguin.com

Acknowledgments to the original publishers of portions of this work appear on page 113.

Frontispiece: Photograph by Colin Doyle

LIBRARY OF CONGRESS CATALOGING-IN-PUBLICATION CONTROL NUMBER: 2016012488
ISBN 9780143108177

Printed in the United States of America
10 9 8 7 6 5 4 3 2 1

Set in Bembo Std
Designed by Elyse Strongin, Neuwirth & Associates

When you look at the environmental data,
the conclusion is inescapable: We're toast.

—T. C. BOYLE

CONTENTS

ORIGINS

Plenty uses America's relationship with wheat and glass—metaphorically speaking, "sheaves of glass"—to explore the country's generous gifts and excesses, entrances and exits.

Wheat and glass are a driving force behind the creation of sedentary, polluting civilizations (no need to move if there are abundant windows, limitless electronic screens, and a plentiful supply of synthesized but toxic bread).

As seeds of the Anthropocene and global warming, wheat and glass are permanently bonded, wedded to each other and to us: sheaves of plenty, sheaves of glass.

I.

Neither glass nor wheat is native to North America.

Glass trade beads were first introduced to Arizona and New Mexico by Francisco Vásquez de Coronado y Luján in 1540. The first North American glass factory was established in Jamestown, Virginia, during 1608.

In 1493 Christopher Columbus brought wheat—an ancient annual grass—to the New World. Hernán Cortés de Monroy y Pizarro carried wheat from Spain to Mexico by ship in 1519. Beginning in 1540, missionaries and conquistadors first took wheat from Mexico to what is now Arizona and California. However, wheat was first grown productively on an island just off the Massachusetts coast in 1602—just six years before construction of the first glass factory in North America.

II.

Glass is a trinity: a mixture of sand (silica), limestone, and soda ash that is heated to an extremely high temperature (1,575° C/2,867° F) and then cooled. Glass furnaces also are tripartite: the first furnace, which contains a crucible filled with molten glass, is called simply "the furnace"; the second, which glassblowers use to reheat pieces while working, is called a "glory hole"; and the last, called the "annealer" or "lehr," gradually cools the glass.

Because it is sticky and viscous, glass only *seems* solid; upon finally reaching room temperature in the annealer, glass behaves like a liquid but actually is an amorphous solid.

• • •

Glass furnaces are perpetual; they must operate 24/7 and cannot be shut down or even partially cooled during their entire fifteen- to eighteen-year life span. Modern glass factories use natural gas and fuel oil (a liquid petroleum product) for heat; both are potent contributors to global warming.

The production of glass creates water pollution and releases huge quantities of carbon dioxide, sulfur dioxide, nitrogen oxides, and toxic dust into the atmosphere. Coating glass to create mirrors and other products results in an assortment of volatile organic compounds.

Roughly 40 percent of glass is defectively manufactured and must be discarded. Glass is one of the primary components of household waste in America. Although infinitely recyclable, glass is one of the most difficult and energy-intensive products to recycle. Americans recycle less than 25 percent of the glass they use.

• • •

It is not possible to remove glass from the environment. In addition, after sand, limestone, and soda ash are melted together, the resulting glass cannot be returned to its separate "origins" as distinct components. Even when glass fragments into tiny grains—a process that takes one million years or more—its three original ingredients remain bound forever, a metaphorical and actual melted sheaf.

Similarly, America cannot be separated from its conflicting roles—as enslaver and emancipator, warmonger and peacemaker, imprisoner and liberator, mass murderer and life giver, exterminator of tribes and advocate for the indigenous, manufacturer of toxic herbicides and preserver of forests, fossil fuel harvester and inventor of alternative energy sources—or from the technologies that enable those roles. Nor can the country be divorced from its rapacious appetites and capacious gifts.

III.

The high-yield dwarf varieties of wheat—introduced during the mid-twentieth century and now widely used—ensure plentiful harvests but also have countless negative impacts, ranging from lost and weak topsoil to bakers who must wear masks because they become allergic to their own flour.

Ancient varieties of wheat are annual grasses that have existed for millennia. Willowy and elegant, they grow tall, which causes them to topple when doused with herbicides and pesticides. Modern engineered dwarf varieties are shorter, sturdier, and able to remain upright after spraying.

. . .

Agribusiness wheat crops are often sprayed with Monsanto's Roundup, a powerful herbicide and desiccant, to kill weeds and facilitate early harvest by prematurely drying grain. The active ingredient in Roundup is a chemical called glyphosate.

"Weeds" and other plants are evolving to resist glyphosate, becoming plentiful "superweeds," such as giant ragweed, that eradicate native flora and fauna.

Monsanto has genetically engineered "Roundup Ready" seeds such as corn, soy, canola, alfalfa, sorghum, and wheat—these plants resist glyphosate and similar herbicides, remaining alive even when native grasses and other plants around them perish after a spraying.

Roundup Ready seeds are nicknamed "Terminator Seeds" because the crops they produce are sterile, so farmers cannot save their best seeds for the next season and are forced to buy seeds from Monsanto on an essentially infinite basis. Monsanto's profits double because farmers must buy both Roundup and Roundup Ready seeds. In some areas of North America, the majority of farmers now have extreme difficulty growing seeds that are not genetically engineered.

In response to widespread opposition, Monsanto withdrew its Roundup Ready wheat from production in 2004. Regardless, almost a decade later, rogue "volunteer" Roundup Ready wheat was found growing in an Oregon field. Despite its promise to end Roundup Ready production, Monsanto has resumed testing Roundup Ready wheat at fields in North Dakota and Hawai'i.

. . .

Roundup's glyphosate residue has been discovered in the tissues and urine of human beings as well as wild and domesticated animals—and in drinking water. It not only causes morphological abnormalities in amphibians, but also dramatically decreases the biodiversity of aquatic communities.

In addition to killing plants, glyphosate destroys bacteria and damages the integrity of soil. One species of earthworm ceases activity following a few weeks of exposure to glyphosate. Other earthworm species' reproduction is halved after exposure to the herbicide.

Glyphosate is sprayed not only on wheat and other crops, but also on home gardens, roadsides, and fields. One of its impacts is an 81 percent decline in monarch butterflies where glyphosate is sprayed, because the chemical destroys milkweed—the only plant monarch caterpillars are able to consume.

The World Health Organization has declared glyphosate to be a probable carcinogen. Chronically ill human beings have higher percentages of glyphosate in their bodies.

Women are particularly susceptible to the effects of glyphosate. Because women have more fatty tissue, they store more of the herbicide (as well as other toxic chemicals) in their bodies. Via the placenta, women pass those toxins to developing fetuses. Women then feed their babies contaminated breastmilk.

. . .

The Union of Concerned Scientists has discovered DNA changes in the traditional seed supply due to contamination by transgenic Roundup Ready seeds.

Ironically, studies have found a correlation between glyphosate and an increase in diseases that affect wheat. In another bizarre turn, Roundup Ready canola has emerged as a devastating superweed that compromises other crops, such as grapes and cotton.

In short, glyphosate ensures plenty—a generous, perpetual harvest of both crops and calamities. It is just one of the countless DDT-DDE-DDDs of our time.

. . .

Modern farming techniques used to grow wheat and other crops are responsible for lasting, widespread environmental damage. Impacts include water pollution and drought (agriculture uses about 70 percent of all available freshwater worldwide); pesticides, herbicides, and fungicides; chemical fertilizers; harvesting, extraction, and bleaching; habitat change; reduction in biodiversity; soil erosion; and emissions from machinery like combines, tractors, trucks, and refrigerators.

Nitrogen fertilizers used in industrial agriculture are the source of more than half of the nitrous oxide in the atmosphere.

. . .

The average American consumes more than 130 pounds of wheat each year.

IV.

My Greiner ancestors and living relatives have been famous German glassblowers for centuries. They were once known for painting poetry on glass.

Jewish and Lutheran immigrants, my Greiner ancestors were also among the first glassblowers in North America.

From an original contract to establish a glass manufacturing facility in New York in 1752:

> . . . I the underwritten Johan Martin Greiner of Saxe Weimar . . . will Embark from Rotterdam for New York in America aforesaid and on my Arrival there shall and will Instruct and Inform in Ev'ry respect . . . in the Art and Mistery of Erecting and Building a Glass House and also in Blowing and Making of Glass. . . .

. . .

All early American glassworks caused deforestation of huge swaths of land because the furnaces needed to be constantly supplied with wood.

Later, when glassworks inevitably closed due to lack of timber, the treeless land was converted to large farms—many of which eventually were used for industrial agriculture, especially in the eastern and midwestern United States.

To survive after their glassworks failed, my ancestors inevitably resorted to large-scale farming of land destroyed by the furnaces' insatiable appetite for trees to burn.

. . .

Many German Jewish Greiners were murdered during the Holocaust. At least one gentile German Greiner—underground resistance fighter and spy Robert Andrew Greiner—was arrested by the Gestapo, sent to Dachau, and then murdered.

Because Greiners have made so much of Germany's glass for centuries, it is certain that some of the glass shattered on Kristallnacht was created by Greiners. Also known as "Crystal Night" or "The Night of Broken Glass," Kristallnacht was the "beginning of the end," a major event in the inception of the Holocaust.

On November 9 and 10, 1938, during the Kristallnacht pogrom, the Nazi Sturmabteilung or SA (Storm Detachment or Assault Division) and non-Jewish civilians (especially Hitler Youth) destroyed Jewish synagogues, homes, and other buildings; cemeteries; and shops. In the process, they smashed so many windows that heaps of broken glass covered the streets.

During these anti-Semitic riots, an estimated thirty thousand Jewish men were arrested and taken to concentration camps. Non-Jewish German officials and civilians were generally passive and did not protect Jewish victims of the riots. Firefighters, for example, worked only to prevent fires from spreading to buildings and homes owned by non-Jews; they allowed Jewish structures, including synagogues, to burn to the ground.

Non-Jewish Germans were described repeatedly as merely "watching" the destruction of Kristallnacht, sanctioning and participating through inaction. Their passivity emboldened Hitler and the Nazi party, and the SA eventually was superseded by the notorious SS.

PREFACE

Plenty uses Walt Whitman's *Leaves of Grass* as a springboard of sorts; however, Whitman's America obviously is not *our* America—post Holocaust, post atomic bomb, post 9/11, post drone, post Roundup, etc. (Whitman himself wrote differently after serving as a Civil War nurse.)

. . .

The first edition of *Leaves of Grass*, a collection of twelve poems, was published in 1855. Whitman revised and added to it throughout his life, and multiple editions were published. The final "deathbed" edition—more accurately called an "impression"—contained 389 poems and was published in 1892. Whitman died two months after preparing it for publication.

Most of the historical material in *Plenty* is focused on America and is from 1892 or later. Although *Plenty* is an epic, it also is meant to resemble a footnote to, or commentary on, *Leaves of Grass*.

. . .

The following events of 1892 have echoes in *Plenty*.

In 1892, more people were lynched in the United States than during any other year in the country's history.

In June 1892, Homer Plessy was arrested for sitting in a "whites only" railway car; the case eventually led to *Plessy v. Ferguson*, which upheld racial segregation through a "separate but equal" doctrine. That law remained in effect for decades, until it was repudiated by *Brown v. Board of Education* in 1954.

The Pledge of Allegiance was created in 1892.

Feminist Charlotte Perkins Gilman's iconic story "The Yellow Wallpaper" was published in 1892.

In 1892, Ellis Island began accepting immigrants into the United States.

Some American glass companies began in 1892 to use molds of actual American coins to make "coin glass." Concerned that the process could be used to make real currency, the government soon deemed the manufacture of coin glass illegal, a form of counterfeiting. The Liberty Head dime also was first minted in 1892. It had a bust of Lady Liberty on the front and a beribboned wreath of wheat sheaves on the back, circling the words "ONE DIME."

The patent for the two-way telegraph was granted to Thomas Edison in 1892.

In 1892, Winchester began making the Winchester Model 1892 rifle. This lightweight gun became one of the most popular weapons in America because it was a repeating, lever-action rifle that fired pistol-caliber rounds. John Wayne used a Winchester 1892 in dozens of films about conquering the West—even though the gun was invented after most of the American frontier had been settled—and the 1892 was featured in many TV shows, such as *The Rifleman*. Today, the Winchester Repeating Arms Company describes the gun as having "impressive strength," "low recoil, and responsive, easy handling."

Field Experiments with Wheat, published in 1892, addressed everything from grain shrinkage in granaries to diseases like "stinking smut" and "scab." Primarily, though, the document focused on ways to increase yields of dozens of wheat varieties, among them Rock Velvet, Bearded Monarch, Wisconsin Triumph, Tasmanian Red, Yellow Gypsy, Extra Early Oakley, Golden Prolific, Badger, and Surprise. In contrast, today's high-yield wheat species, which comprises 95 percent of all wheat grown in America, is called simply Common Wheat or Bread Wheat.

In 1892, the Pawnee of Oklahoma ratified an agreement to accept separate, individual parcels of land and dissolve their communal land holdings.

• • •

Throughout 1892, a group of Americans and Europeans—mostly businessmen—plotted to overthrow Queen Lili'uokalani, the last monarch of Hawai'i. She had become queen only one year earlier. They feared for their business interests and resented the country being led by a woman. Queen Lili'uokalani had written a radical new constitution that restored the monarchy's veto powers and at last provided voting rights to poor, disenfranchised

Hawai'ians and Asians. In addition to her threatening accomplishments as champion of the poor, the queen perhaps intimidated the Americans through her erudition and achievements; she was an extraordinary author, historian, composer, singer, and musician.* When the coup d'état was actualized in 1893, America invaded and deposed the queen. In his State of the Union address later that year, newly inaugurated president Grover Cleveland urged Congress to take an "honorable course" and "undo the wrong," restoring the monarchy. However, the new president of Hawai'i, Sanford Dole (of what later became the famous Dole pineapple dynasty), simply ignored the president's insistence that the queen be reinstated. Dole and others were focused on profiting from industrial agriculture on Hawai'i's highly productive volcanic soil, and they knew that Hawai'i's annexation by the United States meant sales of fruits and vegetables to the mainland would not have import tariffs. Dole Food Company, Inc., is now a multinational corporation, the largest fruit and vegetable producer in the world. Its "Dole Plantation" on Oahu, a popular tourist attraction, receives more than a million visitors a year. Dole Food Company, Inc., also runs "plantations" around the world, and the corporation is often accused of violating workers' rights. Since Dole and others assumed control in the 1890s, many Native Hawai'ians continue to strive for sovereignty, venerate their former queen, and believe they live in occupied territory.

Also in 1892, the founder of the notorious Carlisle Indian Industrial School, Captain Richard Henry Pratt, presented at a convention his lengthy treatise on how to "civilize" and educate "savages." He compared those efforts to "civilizing" African Americans. After the Sioux author Zitkala-Ša wrote an article criticizing those methods for *Harper's Monthly*, she was fired from her teaching position at the Carlisle Indian Industrial School. Zitkala-Ša, who had been educated at the White's Manual Labor Institute—an institution similar to the Carlisle Indian Industrial School—was not only a teacher, but also an accomplished musician, political activist, writer, and editor.

---

* The text used to create the poem's fading image of Queen Lili'uokalani (see page 90) is from her memoir *Hawai'i's Story by Hawai'i's Queen*. The erasure of both text and image is meant to mirror and draw attention to Americans' convenient, continuing, tourist-fueled amnesia regarding Hawai'i's tragic history. As a remedy, readers are encouraged to read her entire memoir and other works. The complete text used to create the image is provided at http://digital .library.upenn.edu/women/ liliuokalani/hawaii/hawaii.html.

In 1892, the African American activist and author Ida B. Wells initiated a crusade against lynching after three friends suffered police brutality, were arrested, and then were murdered by a Memphis mob. (Although the murderers were known to police, they were not punished.) Wells soon became internationally famous for her assertion, supported by research, that lynching in America was primarily a method of punishing blacks for competing with whites, especially in business. Her pamphlet *Southern Horrors: Lynch Law in All Its Phases*, published in 1892, presented her analysis. Together with Frederick Douglass and other black luminaries, Wells led a black boycott of the 1893 World's Fair and helped to author a pamphlet called *The Reason Why the Colored American Is Not in the World's Columbian Exposition* (African Americans were presented at the fair in a racist and dehumanizing manner). Wells was also a suffragist, editor, journalist, book author, and charismatic lecturer.

Lucy Gonzalez Parsons began her periodical *Freedom: A Revolutionary Anarchist-Communist Monthly* in 1892. She was such an effective labor organizer and champion of working-class liberation that the Chicago police called her "more dangerous than a thousand rioters." Gonzalez Parsons, an uncompromising feminist, also organized mothers, housewives, and other women who worked but were not paid for their labor into the Working Women's Union. She was biracial—her parents were of Native American, Mexican, and perhaps African American ancestry—and was persecuted for her marriage to a white man. Albert Parsons, her husband, was shot in the leg and threatened with lynching for registering black voters. He eventually was accused, without evidence, of participation in the 1886 Haymarket strike bombing and sent to the gallows. Even after his death, Gonzalez Parsons remained a fearless advocate for the poor and disenfranchised, organizing the first ever march on Washington, D.C. Equally incensed about income inequality, sexism, and racism, she wrote tirelessly for newspapers and gave speeches all over America before hundreds of thousands of people. Toward the end of her life, Gonzalez Parsons campaigned for the release of the nine African American "Scottsboro Boys," young men egregiously accused of raping two white women—and she maintained her campaign for clemency despite lynch mobs, all-white juries, and rampant hostility. When Gonzalez Parsons was killed in a house fire at age eighty-nine, Chicago police seized her surviving library of three thousand books and research on, according to their description, "sex, socialism, and anarchy" and then gave them to the FBI; her library was never seen again.

SYMBOLOGY

Some symbols in this poem are mathematical, and there are allusions in the epic to sheaf mathematics.

A sheaf is a way to follow data related to a topological space (its open sets). Mathematical sheaves exist in sheaves of rings or sheaves of sets.

Symbols related to sheaf mathematics:

~ The tilde is also called a "swung dash."

   In sheaf mathematics a ~ means "to morph."

   In general mathematics, it is labeled a "twiddle" and shows a relationship between objects.

* The asterisk, also called a "star," has many purposes in mathematics. The most common use is to indicate multiplication. In sheaf mathematics, the star has various uses; one is to show a ring's multiplicative group.

∞ In mathematics, the infinity symbol, or lemniscate, is used to indicate a *potential* for infinity.* Mathematical sheaves can exist in ∞-stacks and other configurations.

Other symbols:

| war, division, separation

V death, ending, the past

---

* There are references in *Plenty* to Vladimir Nabokov's 999-line poem *Pale Fire*. Nabokov used what he called the "miracle of a lemniscate" as a repeated symbol in the poem: "Outstare the stars. Infinite foretime and / Infinite aftertime . . ."

∧	conception, birth, infants, future
<	increasing, expanding
>	decreasing, shrinking
< >	both a beginning and an ending (or an increase and a decrease at once)
> <	transcendence
O	fertility

INCEPTION

. . . it's constructed not of human bodies, as I'd feared,
but rather out of small slivers of glass
in the shapes of bones.

> —G. C. WALDREP, "The Night Autopsy"

Rescued, I see no truth in things. . . .
My child is fed of the first wheat.

> —LOUISE ERDRICH, "Captivity"

How many heartfuls of sorrow shall balance a bushel of wheat?

> —W. E. B. DU BOIS, *The Souls of Black Folk*

Conifers feather and brighten
as darkness.

Herons clap
their seed rattles.

Elastic, my new grass skirt
unpeels and whinnies.

Black bread, pearl gherkins.
Clotted butter.

Cautiously naked,
I neither form nor close.

But the gods enter
me and drop

a river————
————that streams
in the shape

of this Holi parade ~ Brooklyn   curry breeze

tossing rainbow talcum
powder at hennaed children

who spray turquoise *Gulal* back

until we pull coiled cords
and the Hindu dancers' masks open <
revealing second   no, endless   inner beings

who desire not
an invocation

but a coagulation . . . .

                 . . . . not *to* a muse
               but *with* a fuse . . . .

. . . . because that's all
that's left among
the diapersspituprattlesmacbooksonesiesremoteslaundry————

No twelve books here, the dancers say—

            our souls   epic   but erotic
                                                not periodic—

         inclined to dissipate
         and ramble like wind————

Let us wander then   ~   *away*
to our Mojave . . . . drifts   to desiccate . . . .

occipital/saguaro
fallopian/ocotillo—

our breaths in and on the playas:
greasewood
sagebrush
thymus & thyme—

datura binds scapula   our seepwillow *vas*
deferens   hip dewthrust
your labia now fringed   with dozens

of reef-blue eyes
like a Florida bay
scallop—

A few more piercings | a few routs | a reaching

                              round
                              of sharpened
                              limbs |

                                 wet red slick—
                                 of menstrual broth?—

Flesh tears on the yucca, creosote————

     Come, bandage me   with your hair
     and sweetmilk ejaculate

                  of tarbush————

————*but there is no remedy*

because America displays living
Apache and Mbuti
as exhibits

at the Saint Louis World's Fair

human zoo
dubbed *The University of Man*————————

thus our New World   false
nationmother   pregnant

knits

eves
at her home in winter—Nebraska—

hot bricks to warm the bed
scent of venison stew   /   woodstove smoke
weight the air

for months she knits
for her unborn

needles *2mm*

booties+overalls+cardigans+caps

handspun   pale jade   wine and ivory

and afghans that—as time unfurls—

form
trains+autos+jets+machineguns+laptops————

at last
sudden daffodils of spring

then her broken water
in the uncovered wagon——

and soon her firstborn   a crying son——

                              but *she bleeds out*

husband cradles her——weeps   her fading

                                        pulse drum

                    she bleeds out   dark matter

she bleeds out   a world . . . . worlds

of string and
strings

                    she bleeds out

thrashing beneath clotted
sheets   she says   *I Didn't Birth*
                                            My Boy
                                            To Be a Soldier

breath ends |

and still | *She bleeds out*————————

————into

America's Motorcycle Church
of the Savior,

where a fricassee of
quail testicles—hollowtipped bullets—crushed amber—metal knuckles—
oystershells—methoxychlor—ginseng—phthalates—arsenic—musk—

if applied daily, will straighten just about any
bent penis

                              (but after you slap
                         me,
                              my love for you
                                   breaks apart

                    like a capsule—

                              then you say,
                              a grenade in the hand
                              is worth more

                              than two in the bush)

dats rite!
agrees our president
while reading a goat book
                    to children
                    as all towers burn———

               death of birth
birth of death
               birth of death
death of birth———

                         now the McIntosh
                         apples, engineered with verve,
                         sprout thick
                         pubic hair
                         tonsures
                         around their stems

Don't touch me there———

———where America out of the cradle
is endlessly flocking
           for *The People, Yes*———

———her hunger
for *more* always
a cracking plexi
glass

contract—since we did
not predict our children

would kill their children
when the crops failed.

America a chilled silicone breast,
winged, wearing
a lead-powdered

shutup wig, streams blood
that turns into snakes
as she flies. She orders

Go West, young woman ~ young man, be native!
Grow up with this country
And our wheat—
And our glass—

What is a native?
A native is a what?

Go West, she says, *sing of alarms*
and of endangered
and of extinct
kin—

and of flight————

————to Summits of the Sierras
then Snake River
into Utah's Valley

of Babbling Waters
as Yosemite's Bridal Veil Falls—

Now the Great Salt Lake.
Trailing tears.

All I ask in this creation
Is a pretty little wife
And a big plantation
Way up yonder in the Cherokee Nation—
$1.25 per acre!

Six months by oxen wagon train
From Independence, Missouri, to San Francisco, California————

Last Cut, Big Fill, Chinese
Workers on the railroad—
Shoshone forced to beg
At stations of the train—

Navajo Long Walk, the old the young dying
All for telegraphofficebargroceryblacksmithderricks——

Locomotives crashing
Into Mesa Verde? The Smartphone
Wedding to Deepwater Horizon?   Suspicious

                    Are the children, who ask,

                    Once the gods have whispered,
                    who are we to alter it?——

But we do not think
of what the gods have whispered——

——so all we can offer

        are

        TED Talk
        topics——

To build dinosaurs from chickens is an antidote for apathy
And aligns our past and present personae

Our bodies are haunted by lost masses of polar ice
Yet can share things learned when drones crash

Organic gardens will fuel the smallest 3D printer
In ignorance of what you learned before birth

Wireless data avoids the origins of pleasure
Fearing stories etched on paper are the real reason for brains

Few are aware that bond markets can keep streams flowing
While turning trash into toys for learning

Discount nuclear fuel does not trust poems
And wonders, Can't we make things that make themselves?

Spider silk explains how to defend Earth from asteroids
And discerns ways for plankton to charge batteries

Meet the dancing ballbot, with a prosthetic nose that smells
The global power shift into fighting contagious cancer

Silicon-based, these digital clams tour dunescapes
And dare to ask, Are we filtering the wrong bacteria?

A green school gives lessons from karaoke champions
On instructing rats to sniff out land mines

Big brands save biodiversity by wiring an interactive ocean
Based on knowing pork bellies make the world turn

Those who grow new organs kindly make a park in the sky
And welcome we suicide attempt survivors who tassel out, thrive——

——yet from our gaps protrudes something
that looks like leaves——but is not————

Kristallnacht   world divided
                    into two broken parts:

>   **1**   *places where*
>   *we cannot live*
>
>   *and*
>
>   **2**   *those*
>   *we cannot enter* . . . .

. . . . so on the Ho Chi Minh trail
a flushed rose Memphis gunner
raises hand to heart pocket—

                    his fingers   push   into
Marlboros | marrow | blood—
glass syringe snaps
in the medic's shudder~hand

He was binding sheaves, the gunner's widow wails . . . .
In the field . . . . tying together . . . .

But his sheaves stood up, separate . . . .
The others bowed to them . . . .
Followed without thought . . . .

and then >   *a fusing* >
and then >   *a shattering* >   =   *America*————————

where everything's a mission field
and the prophet is an armadillo, no,

the prophet is polyvinyl chloride pulling
the kiss, like taffy,

to breaking >

yeah I Like America and America Likes Me but
watch for images of flags and targets sparking

on découpaged newsprint
and those fracking music boxes that if opened

play flaming

tin recorded sounds of their offshore
mating in the modern supermarket

one tends to deny that shrink
wrapped pork and porcupine taste

the same if stewed with DDT-DDE-DDD and
ovicidesalgicidesmiticidesnematicidesrodenticidesbiocidesmolluscicides

therefore on deserted

beaches I make love aggressively yet baroquely
brooms blooming for thousands still burned

as Teachers and Midwives and Doulas and Witches
in this Christian Era,

their ashes warning,

Beware, you lookers,
Annie Oakley could shoot

flames

off candles
as they rotated

on a wheel

because she knew *it's womb envy not the
other* and she blocked gods with her flame
retardant paint thinner dry cleaning fluid
toilet deodorizer dioxin rocket fuel
breastmilk-bloodmilk but hey not to
worry every blessed Native has been
presented with an automobile spiked with
aluminum nails and titled *Gift* look we
stitched together a heartwarming collage
of "found" video clips from Guantanamo
surveillance cameras at Camp *X-Ray if
everyone is the police where do we survive*
another corporal leashes his prisoners so
without question *I Want You whispers Uncle
Sam* cozily our handshake amputated at the
wrist *of course disposable picnic blankets are a
necessary perk of Amerika* but in the capital we
were born with *brain tumors that began in vitro
who knows it might be the water* **they say** and
venereal are the buried laws who sing of
sharp sea glass and wave after wave of
Gitmo at last rounding into Monsanto *
Syngenta * DuPont * Dow grain to feed
the best hinds of our enervation harping
hypothetical strafed lagging note how in
every attic mothers keen bulging like pin-
cushions with fiberglass filaments and
carboniferous agrochemical ~ petrochemical
pinspinspinspinspinspinspinspinspinspins
pinspinspinspins————

————and mermaid tears————
————seeping————weeping————

————in fear of our last Roundup Ready Rodeo

where we,
the audience,
ascend from burning

vinyl briefcases
and BPA baby
bottles. Our bleacher

smoke twists, coils,
and does not dissipate
but remains as grit

that abrades teeth
into nothing. See the cow
boys and cow

girls mount
their Holocene dung

beetles because

there are no
more horses—riders
must diet

for decades,
shrinking
into dried peas

with arms and legs
like whiskers. See the wo
men

rodeo
clowns forced
to give birth

from their
urethras—infants
like goji berries,

hairless, wrinkled
dry and raw
pink. Their fathers kiss

    those tiny dead
    on the cheeks, sobbing,
    caressing,

    but when
    we at last run
    to comfort, even to stop

    them, we find only hollowed
    comb, mites, and sticky—
    so sticky—

        honeyyellow
        amberyellow

        shit——

    ——warning against now,

when all gel-swaddled
frog eggs

can't unmix

from our parasite-
atrazine spill.

So our flowers begin
to fly apart

at their edges, torn
by bees

without tongues.
This thick

and newly splattering
breath.

Our locked clam thoughts.

I run to inquire,
yet you pause apart.

Suddenly what we love
is no longer morning

to our lawn's green throats.

Then one frog displays legs
in threes, sixes, even nines.

They grow from its mouth:
silence————

and from our mouths: *silence*————

and from *this* silence————

       that is combed from night-black lanugo like damp
       swamp grass on my stillborn daughter who warns
       through sewn mouth that after seeding into your
       tongue genetically engineered common wheat

       < can grow and produce dun nurse moths who bring >

       eternal boxed Chablis as spring bulbs plan to uncork
       other women my viper choir stands jealous on tidal
       tails then distant hens acquire my live child portion
       see for months after stillbirthing how mourning skins
       me on a fall tree always an apple like me too deep or too

       high for picking over time its skin browns shines
       collapses in puckers as if something is eating from
       within note that shortly before death Miró wanted to
       make sculptures out of gas he knew some snowflakes
       sublime instead of melt as they transition from solid to
       gas without the liquid stage without the stage of liquid

       like my still born / born still darling look at my
       blood bubbles backed up in the morphine pump
       ashe junipers just outside the maternity-morgue
       ward window flap-slapping their prickle branch
       wings cloudy with copper gone pollen well-well
       my gone baby could you tell me quickly completely

*whichtoxin whichtoxin whichtoxin whichtoxin whichtoxin
whichtoxin whichtoxin whichtoxin whichtoxin whichtoxin
which———————*

did this?

|perfluorinatedcompoundspolybro
minateddiphenylethersphthalatesdi
chlorodiphenyltrichloroethanepoly
chlorinateddbenzodioxinsglyphosa
tebromoxynilphenolspolycyclicaro
matichydrocarbonsmercuryperfluo
rooctanoicacidvinclozolinMSGurani
um235?|

No answer
except: *we turn on the kitchen
                 tap and flames come out———*

hothotterhottest! hothotterhottest! hothotterhottest!

                 gee better be careful
                 your house could explode———

hothotterhottest! hothotterhottest! hothotterhottest!

                 and don't water the carrots
                 they could become vectors———

hothotterhottest! hothotterhottest! hothotterhottest!

| ah baby are you still born mis carried still? |

———look now   !ooh!   through the cheesecloth
ozone   the steaming   eagle   has landed
  on the megalopolis turnpike   wide enough for
semis   missile trucks   tanks
          prison vans   station wagons———

———wheeling past ready wheat
                 fields drenched
                 in dazzling
                 Roundup—

then past cleverly confined
animal
feeding operations—

and Jonah's gas
field, with a fiberglass
whale photo op—

behind festive fracking
flowback
pit stops————

————and so we fear this screed of scree:

As bats lose home
and fish gills stiffen   warming, warming—
our hunger hardens
to a graspish Devonian

jig. Yakety yak, few talk
back and most rasp, grating forth

a decree: Come, warm as the dead,
let's pick the bat-fish

from our breath like swill—

and eat
and eat————

because anything
can be made

into sushi—   even the Gray Bat
                               even the Spotted Ratfish—

into karaoke—   even Tower
                               even Cage—

mmm hmm   yes   let's eat
                     and eat————

————this candy striped
Exxon sea cucumber, which shoots

poisonous sticky threads
from its anus—

the confused
sea sponge studding
itself with discarded
cruise ship lollipops—

the box jellyfish that intones
like an entrailed
Big Mac cathedral:
Eat or thou shalt be eaten—

the coelacanth chewing
on its fins, tasting
liquid
smoke   benzene   beef—

the petroleum carpet
on ocean's surface
that laments dispersants
then invents ChapStick—

the CO_2 birthing acid sea
water stiletto crabs
already spawning
triplets—

        the glass diatoms, who say,

        It does not matter
        if we sink or float—

        but if our clear
        true houses break: *Death*———

———*Death,* I say, too,

led by my
unholy books

called *The Birds of Self-Knowledge,*

my false field guides, guide fields

that I dream
as I read———

SCREECH OWL OF FRIGATES
———of robust
herbed

Walmart PSYOP
croutons

approaching, armed,
from the north

sea—in defense,
they explain,

calm down
all consciousness
is comprised
of minute
children

WARBLER OF PUNJAB
who watch
me channel James Joyce
        before breakfast,

but then he chooses
            to honor
the yapping electric
poodle toy   massive

plankton die-off, coral
reefs   bleaching,

        rooftops   beneath rising   sea—

my genital pendula
tick-tock   if,

upon waking,
you notice   a rat

has been gnawing
          at your underwear,
do not attempt

any profound
                    activities   Ibegofyou

                                              find me corn silk, bottled

queen's breath   ganesh to help

                              this soul again
                              become
                              a swimming
                              place

BOBOLINK OF SCIENCE MUSEUMS

ancient maps   of the world
featured   sea monsters
wax models   of fetuses
in wombs   beware
a holy whore   the equation
of look   and lack
Shelley's heart   did not burn
in the funeral   pyre
so we hoarders   kept it
for millennia   sealed
in vacuumed   plastic

TANAGER OF CARAPACE
     command these maidservants
             to fulfill duties
             of the kushti   rites

we sell fish morels chestnuts
                  by the roadside
     give birth to children
of soldier   rapists
     in the forests   solace
        solely in dining

                             on old velvet

            organic   pullets
   so: we find
some aardvarks
      ! who fall in love with us !
    then at last
      we are happy

GROSBEAK OF NIGHTSHADE

                  The ghost—
                  hands sheathed
                  in red gloves—

pulls me to
the saline   of his chest

                  knee
                  caps of a sea troll

                  apple
                  from a pippin fairy's tree

             I want love
             but fear
             it won't erase
enough   ozone
from the fresh
lightning strike   observe
             how I curse
             his infidelities
             but disregard

my own   phoenix
talons and Pegasus
feathers   come

                              across the drip–
                              drip glaciers:

                              liberate the mind
by any   means

                              necessary

HAWK OF MOONSTONES
afterthreenightswithoutsleepIcatchmyvaginadentatabarrelingdownthehighway

ALBATROSS OF HEREAFTER
factory farm
        fecal plumes
in this water

tenterhooks
        of terminator
seeds

so on my plate you mix
        crossroads dirt
        goblin teeth
        moss from a hobling's foot
        a black snow goose

Oh Wolf, I am counting
on your megastore, which welcomes
we shoplifters
        like fruit

to fetch   our bones
        from The World
        Afire

HUMMINGBIRD OF BERM
IN MY FIRST CAVE ALWAYS
A PAWKY DRAGONLADY
SWEEPING HER EYES
NARROW DONTCHA
KNOW WARM WATER
DONT DISSOLVE
CO_2 SO WELL OH YEAH
IM DAMN TIRED BUT
I AINT GOIN DOWN

MOORHEN OF DHARMA
Like that icon I can weep from my sternum

     And on particularly tragic days
     From the left thumb

TITMOUSE OF TABERNACLE
Round babyfeet
Robin bloom
Squirrel angles
Violet crumbs

So pause the vacant
wheel   and parch
           winds:

Because still
there is wordless
rose.

COOT OF OUTLANDS
Your fez   could be a marriage
        I do accept faux armor
   but feh   it is not worth

   as many goblin points

                        narwhal

horn   fashioned
            of resin

                        are there more
                        like you

that have never seen

                                    daylight?

WREN OF CINDER
Not riddled with just nine syl
lables. In the beginning Red King
Ted felt me up then it was good
but I failed to notice his label, UNTHINK :
SHRINK. Thus his matter snuck
in—because The All barks wet. So cosmic
wonders won't lessen their rabbit hole geography.
Like: Kabul's finally gone queer! Clouds fellate zeppelins!
With these barrowful breasts, I'm wink sure of nothing but
custard and sighing. Can't tame the squeaky happy baby thing,
always busy in me with its fine squirming. Done footsteps won't
revise. Motherhood refuses the bellglass, Dos Passos: instead
a bell jar for all hearts, all time. See, cinder plus glue make
wheatglass glinder. Slickwater plus proppants make
bedrock tremble. Roundup plus flesh make
teratogen tinder.
Fuckedfrackedfuckedfrackedfucked?

BUZZARD OF MERGE
can't help wishing
        every grown soul
        had love
        leaking
        from its mouth—

so stop
driving, you drivel

dribblers: *THE FORESTS*
                    ARE BURNING

OSPREY OF RAT-A-TAT-TAT BAM-BOOM
Reborn as glass dew
that falls chiming,

bleeding with cautions. Founder the winged

horses. Every saint

is a rind. Sleeping
American *All*
leans West, toward

M16, AC-556, M4A2
locked and loaded—
albatross

after albatross tumbling
until ground rises
in dead thickets

of feather snow—

but our harridan
atoms refuse
to shovel—

screeching
in mourning

for SandyHookVirginiaTechColumbine
cafeteriashallwaysclosetsoverturneddesks—

> *Thou tellest*
> *my wanderings:*
>
> *Put thou my tears*
> *In thy glass bottle:*
>
> *Are they not in thy book?*

JUNCO OF SKUNK MUSK

In the Hindu magic mirror my astral influence and occult magnetism
perceive America devour her children denying

that the inclinations of friendship are in all fruits and vegetables

Shetland pony hoof parings tossed with marigold diapers and nipple
shields carpet our marriage bed pie tin of glow-

worms fizzling *be wise as a*
serpent the frozen macaroni and cheese says softly

but harmless as a dove————

FORK-TAILED STORM PETREL OF ELEVATION

The gods designed Woman while sipping
QWIKSERV:

    like a camel,
        two humps in front, two in back—

                                  we are able to survive
                                  for decades

        on wormwood
        stored there—

Yet from down here, although dark,
    I hear wind above
    in the vaulted nova

                                    of cobalt
will claw high, unpolished
                to reach there   to meet
other reanimated
        dames and bathe

                                    in our sheen—

Pssst, I'm your original   U.S. of A.
                         First Lady

GRACKLE OF TATER TOTS

On Sunday disgorge
a balloon

veinous and gristled
like a heart

won't take my children
to Disneybland

because I don't like speaking
to other moms

only fig trees
pink blue yellow

Caribbean houses
are permitted

TURTLEDOVE OF SPAWN

   these nipples are receptors
    for alien
      intelligence whimpering

 today my cosmos demands
to complete
    a life cycle small
      species require less
 than one zinnia
carcass to survive   remember
    how sepia
 tiktaalik tasted
    like chicken well

done evolution depends
   on pubic graybeards
      like us love roe

dearest iguanodon   time to go
    astral

EAGLE OF RECREATIONAL VEHICLES
peyote rickshaw
we can Ouija your links
to Al-Qaeda

> *With each soul*
> *Are sent*
> *Into the world*
> *A guardian*
> *And an accusing angel*

with pinfeathers
of a gryphon lickerish

> LISTEN CHILD:
> Even dinosaurs covered
> Up their shit
> Like cats

PELICAN OF HOKEY POKEY
all tree frogs hiding, afflicted,

in calabashes make

your offerings now

the ancestors are coming

FLICKER OF NAPOLEON'S BRITCHES
The Flowmaster
And his pruney anus

Have absconded
Wire pulled

Through my heart
If there is not enough to eat

They sniff paint
Thinner

This summer
Of solitude

I notice
Other women's toes

Alpine shrubbery growing
Between my teeth

WOODPECKER OF AMNIOCENTESIS
similar to most
modern packages
my label reads
tear at notch
parenthetical Mama
there are beatitudes but also
there is summer squash
noggin del fuego
alien Halloween poly
costumes are always
too warm so
fumigate
the baby
then retreat
with saffron
coriander
unguent
of beeswax
and nutmeats
hey check
out my visionary
pawtucket sluice
these lies are tiny
and neat

GOOSE OF HEGEMONY

In protest   while watching
little ones

in the park

we use french fry remainders salamanders
and sandbox mud

to fashion   earthen sculptures of ourselves
gravid

in poses of ancient goddesses

PARROT OF CRY IT OUT

What do you like to eat, Il Duce?

I eat mermaids.

Sorry, none here.

What do you like to kiss?

I kiss Barbies.

Sorry, only babies here.

Wailing,

unclothed—like pink

cords of wood—
our Accutane

infants are piled
for him

in birdcages,
the tiny doors

fastened.

ORIOLE OF DELECTATION

imports   of   salvia

pomegranates

LOON OF ABJECT

oceans flee	before	me
apologies	in the	gobi
petunias issue	from my	haunches
sure, I believe	in chastity	(for shades)
yearn	to fix you	in aspic
chain	meatier	than link
make nice	will o' wisp	tulle
no telling	our day	before death

SHRIKE OF PEPTIDES

The largest animals

are also the gentlest—

Even though headlines read,   *Hulking*

Arctic Monsters

Run

Amok!

and runny agate   icebergs

are torn asunder—

Find it here, in me, then—

the largesmall

made benign—

newborn grass

piercing

the black

and moldering

stacks

of hay

on my glass cliffs——

and cantering

within

are ten thousand

                wild

horses—

               Yet only I=
                  Can drink=

                  Their milk————

————except a child, not thirsty, says,

What is America's glass?

fetching it for me with nicked hands,

knowing things speak
if looked through
not shattered———

How could I answer the child?

I do not know what it is
any more than anyone.

Those who know, do not say >
Those who say, do not know >

When Kali rises
from the bayou—

her marshgrass dreads
threaded with gasping

infant redfish,
gummed with dispersants, tar—

we ask her what it means.
Sighs she, *Which of you knoweth the perfume of a magnolia?*

We claim that we know.

She strokes pocked furrows
of swamp tupelo bark. Then orders, hissing imperiously,

* Put it into words. *

We cannot.

We are silent————————

                  as water moccasins raise
                  their heads in alarm, popping
                  cloacae in-out
                  to warn:
                  tick ∨ *tick* ∨ *tick*   *(sss sss sss)*   *tick* ∨ *tick* ∨ *tick*
                  · · · — — — · · ·

————————*Shut my eyes,* she says. *Tamp dark*
the bloodroot
sockets.

We cannot.

We make fists, digging

fingernails
into palms————————

She pulls up
a Great Blue
Heron choking

on BP tar
balls
then strangles the bird

with one sharp twist. *Eat it,* she commands,
lifting the corpse

above her head.
Know it.

We do not.

We tremble as our canoes
are tipped

by Letiche the Monster, our Tainted Keitre,
shouting *Who say dey gonna beat da Parish?*

We don't know.

Is it us?

Is it them?

Is it our VP, diverting hospital
power to Colonial

Pipeline
needs?

We don't know.

So we miss
each empty

evacuation
school bus

and fall to float
on shattering glasswater ~

bloodwater,
bumping

Katrina's muttering,
bobbing

dead—————

—————To Guess   To Speculate   To Guess—————

I guess the glass must be all the children
of America   who do not sleep
on cypress moss pallets
to gain strength
from the trees———

I guess it must be Pele's Hair—
          volcanic   windspun—
     each golden glass strand tipped
          with one black tear———

Or Maine's moon jellyfish—
    see-through saucers—
        dustpink gonads   like four-leaf clovers
           in each buttermilk center———

Or fixed lightning   fulgurite—
hollow tubes
      of glass   smooth within   blackrough without
        like Appalachia miners———

I guess it must be the sand of my disposition,
out of clear hard grains melted—
on this strange American ground.

                  I guess it must be Manhattan
        Project Trinitite———gloss-crackle desert crust
                      V

             the sand grains drawn up
                  V

      into the mushroom   ing cloud   melted
                    V

   becoming   celadon   rust   and pitch
                    V

           and then rained down
                  as shards—

                as glass———

———Or I guess it is the Cup of the Gods,
A cloudless goblet deliberately dropped
Bearing no name so that we may seek

Among the sharpness,
Bloodflesh and say *Whose?*———

    Or perhaps we will taste it
    on the someday
    when our armies'

straight, drab uniforms at last
stop hardening stiff and instead cling,
loose untied states

morphing into flexing peignoirs—
lace pulling
across boxy guts,

spaghetti straps gripping
sprung bristle (a holiness

in satin,
and in love, that craves a give~

a bend~   an anarchy
                 of gender)—<

                              O, how our mouths
                         will then laugh, sighing,
                              Come away with us,

                         newloves. The moon's a glass
                                   apple—salty
                         upon our tongues————

————Perchance the glass is the clearbone
Erase~space of our pointillist flesh—

Each atom more than a million times
Smaller than a hair
And more than 99.9999% void—

Or earth/atmosphere's finite but clarion water—
Waste product of star
Formation, some drops older than the sun————

Or I suppose the glass is itself a grain.

          > the produced babe
          of the cosmos ∞ stars ∞ earth ∞ stones ←—

Or I guess it is a uniform rune——
And it means, *Ground among gods among*   *birthwardeath*
                                                           dunedunghumus,

Silica of boneligamenthairteeth

Transparent, the iridescent
Glass eyes
In our loinsnipplesnavels

Jeweling our wombs from inside——<

Sinless, the bare window

And stainless breath————

————But not innocent, the lens
of this formula-fed babe

                              after drinking up

                              Similac-rum sludge
                              we stewed from

·   ·   ·

| INGREDIENTS:

CORN
SYRUP
SUGAR
MILKPROTEIN
ISOLATEHIGHOLEIC
SAFFLOWEROIL
SOYOILCOCONUTOIL
GALACTOOLIGOSACCHA
RIDES. **LESS THAN 2% OF:**
CC.COHNIIOILMALPI
NAOILBETACAROTENELU
TEINLYCOPENECALCIUMPH
OSPHATEPOTASSIUMCITRA
TEPOTASSIUMCHLORIDE
SODIUMCITRATEMAGNESI
UMPHOSPHATEASCORBICA
CIDCALCIUMCARBONATEC
HOLINECHLORIDEFERROUS
SULFATEMAGNESIUMCHLO
RIDEASCORBYLPALMITATE
CHOLINEBITARTRATETAUR
INEMINOSITOLDIALPHATO
COPHERYLACETATEZINC
SULFATEMIXEDTOCOPHER
OLSLCARNITINENIACINAM
IDECALCIUMPANTOTHENA
TEVITAMINAPALMITATECUP
RICSULFATETHIAMINECHLO
RIDEHYDROCHLORIDERIB
OFLAVINPYRIDOXINEHY
DROCHLORIDEFOLICACID
MANGANESESULFATEPOTAS
SIUMIODIDEPHYLLOQUINO
NEBIOTINSODIUMSELENATE
VITAMIND$_3$CYANOCOBALAM
INPOTASSIUMHYDROXID
EANDNUCLEOTIDES(ADENOS
INE5'MONOPHOSPHATECYT
IDINE5'MONOPHOSPHATE
DISODIUMGUANOSINE5'MON
OPHOSPHATEDISODIUMURI
DINE5'MONOPHOSPHATE).

CONTAINS MILK INGREDIENTS. |

—so the first miscarry does not surprise and dead the baby
rests always in my polymeric sheepskin-lined pocket hearse
then we realize we weren't made for walleyed wallstreet
but for the humus mound and must speak not in roadrace
but solely in Nature's languages of dahlia and ova

> now broken
> the transparent
> glassnight
> that lies
> between Heart
> and Reaper

> Dear Loves *I am cold*
> *I am cold*

whole towns withdrawn—
our future a gourding
jacket of rotten
vegetable weep—

later we learn those formulas made in Asia promise only
fatal operations so after the second fetus dies of melamine
and sugar we tumble surrounded by baby showers like
cakes on platforms with egg white icing that seems hard
until pushed and crumbles into our twinges saying copies
of the dead uh no sorry for your loss dear copies of the
babies are not possible

> *are brides just gearshifts are brides just gearshifts*
first baby made a sound
between a lark
and a vole

> *are brides just gearshifts are brides just gearshifts*
second baby scent
of toffee
autumn straw and brine

are brides just gearshifts are brides just gearshifts

slip the miss——carried
down our brooks

on ball moss beds in shy   vellum canoes
       to dip to sink to rest
dusk-lit by bluebell glow
worm lanterns

            underwater

First child gone—
Second child gone—
     Where   *have you two fallen?*
     Why   *have you two fallen?*

   Tell me
     whichtoxinwhichtoxinwhichtoxinwhich
     PBDE?PCB?*brownfield*TCDD?CFH?
     *brownfield*MTBE?DDT?*brownfield*
  did this——?

Again we turn
on the kitchen tap
and flames come out——then water tasting of diesel
       with just a touch
     not harmful surely not harmful
         of benzene——

——Quick: give
up a Liberty Head
dime——because just one
     call to the gods will do:
But only gods who are as fixed
as mountains can fix this.
          Oops, they're out for a Coke
       and cocaine, not back until——

——the tribe-told
unison drum has healed
these wounds that exhale

Red-red-red bird, the chosen daughter
Zitkala-Ša, her tears eating

and her truth voice building
the mountains—she knows
a badger's in the twisting

closed weeds
of late September

glass shards beneath moccasins
wigwams withdrawing ragged
arms into the West—

Istokmus wacipo, tuwayatunwanpi
kinhan ista nisasapi kta:
Dance you must with eyes closed.
Dare to open eyes,
forever red eyes shall have————

————*before the Quaker's apples,*

Mother of Zitkala-Ša was a nestled feast—

every hunger
had breasts for a face—

draped hair
and shone robes with mouths
of understand, the fringed

prairies bundled and kindled—
fired coffeepot, unleavened
bread for visiting

happy uncles
of the finding ground
and great-great-grandfather story——

Dakota daughter

with black
and yellow striped
beaded wolves

on her assembling
thread—

trees shifted soft
against her shoulders,

drummers sat fat
sermons of dance

in precious quiver
of *if . . . then*—

neighboring
of the wind———

———*then, after the Quaker's apples,*

Mother crying her sun on all warrior sons———

Newly cemented land,
the soft white
batting, girdled
pioneer plasticlace dogma—

Missionary teepees exploding,
settler blankets
of boiled-until-bloodless sympathy—

The Forever of It. Shrieking
whistle roots braiding
shoulders poison-beaked,

spirit long walk into steel, cousin———

Thus was howl
snarled in legend———

      ———*those Settler steps won't sand over, yes,*
      their steps   won't sand over———

———to Oklahoma———
Choctaw *okla humma*————"land of the red people":

Enters our Pawnee chief, 1892   earrings clapping
scalp lock and porcupine roach
buckskin war shirt
bottleglass bead bolo

he watches
starving settlers gather

logs!twigs!hay!leaves!sunflowerstalks!clover!buffalochips!
typewriters/PCs/tablets!
magiclanterns/film/VHS/DVD!
cotton/nylon/polyester!
LPs/cassettes/CDs!
punchcards/papertape/magnetictape/floppydisks/harddisks/USBsticks!
V-1s/V-2s/ICBMs!

to build him a fire———

Fools, he says,   *Build a big fire*
And have to get a
Long ways from it.

(hothotterhottest!)

But we build a little fire
And sit around it.

I rise in straw hat / rope suspenders   a pioneer child
to greet him:
Chaticks-si-Chaticks   The "Men of Men"

I this girl or boy
speckled and seeping
bubonicplague∨smallpox∨polio∨ebola∨spanishflu∨MRSA∨SARS

vest pockets bulging with jerked buffalo

stiff as bone for chewing

—he pities me—

so together we hand sickle
all day   barefoot
pants rolled high
whistling through the wheat fields

one tin cup   <   we share
the water crock

and cracked old cornpone
honeycomb
crab apple compote

from my tin lunch pail—→

after I beg
he helps me to bind the field~leavings

                                    of

        | biscuitsnoodlescakesbreadscerealpastacookiesbeer

        blightsofleafrustglumeblotchspindlestreaknodorum |

—and we make glass
shard gravel————→

————beneath Der Führer   who admired
        the efficiency   of our stockades
        for Native Americans   and modeled
        his camps   on our U.S. of A.
        genocide   mastery————→

Heil IBM's Hollerith   Machine
Heil   its precise   tabulations
                                  calculations
                                  ministrations
                                  negations

                                  countingpunchingcounting
                                  punchingcountingpunching

Eh, Friedrich?
"population politics, based
on the principles
of racial hygiene,
must promote valuable
genetic stock"

countingpunchingcounting
punchingcountingpunching

And Heil, no,
Pledge
Allegiance

To our World War   chemicalinnovations
                                     of synthetic

fertilizersweaponspesticidesherbicidesmedicines————>

Heil now, Der Führer, Herr Wolf,
uncurtain the night, allow
pitch glass to hang

our reflections
over the grass———

Then come now, Der Führer, Herr Wolf,
to Terminator Seed
your same glass

shard gravel again————————

          beneath the African-American Sheriff
          cutting down
          the lynched
          Chinese workers—still alive!—who blink, inhale,

          pull up their pants, and descend
          with jump-start hearts
          from where they were hung—
          carriage shop awning, lumberyard gate, covered wagon—

astenthousandwatchastenthousandwatchastenthousandwatch

on *Calle de los Negros*, Los Angeles. The Sheriff invites
eleven lynched New Orleans
Sicilians to resurrect, too,
and hundreds of lynched Gold Rush Mexican miners,

who fashion 24k crowns
bejeweled with NorthCarolinaemeraldsArkansasdiamonds
MontanasapphiresVirginiagarnetsNevadaopals

astenthousandwatchastenthousandwatchastenthousandwatch

for everyone
who was strungburneddismembered

astenthousandwatchastenthousandwatchastenthousandwatch

No untermensch   the Sheriff says—
No other—   until, agitated, he begins
                           to run—

Quickly, quickly!   he bellows.   *A Crucible*
                                                of hothotterhottest!

                                                The ice
                                              is melting. The seas

                                              are climbing. The water
                                              gates cannot

                                              be closed. Starving
                                              are the polar

                                              bears you see swimming
                                              at us

                                              as, openmouthed,
                                              we drown————

then he cuts down the thousands of

BlacksMexicansItaliansChinese
EastIndiansJewsNativeAmericans

—still alive!—
from their lynching
trees and takes a photograph
of them all together, celebrating New

Year's Eve with a grand meal of hog maw, chitterlings,
collard greens, and Hoppin' John filled
with new dimes. The Sheriff turns
that picture into a postcard

astenthousandwatchastenthousandwatchastenthousandwatch

and mails it to us, with only *1892*
written on the back
in bloodied charcoal script——

(we receive it and then lose it
in Paris, Texas, on February 1, 1893)————

————But still we write back:

> *How can we escape the fused—the fired—*
> *—like a patient euthanized—*

> Repeat:
> *How can we escape the fused—the fired—*

> *that which can't be separated*

> *or repaired?————*

> *How can we cross————(speechless)*

. . .

POLICE LINE DO NOT CROSS POLICE LINE DO NOT CROSS

I can't breathe.
Don't shoot.
Mom, I want to go to college.
I want to go home.
I don't want to die.
I can't breathe.

POLICE LINE DO NOT CROSS POLICE LINE DO NOT CROSS

FREEZE!

MOVE!

FREEZE!

POLICE LINE DO NOT CROSS POLICE LINE DO NOT CROSS

How can we *cross*————(breathless)————

————*Welcome to Lockdown Amerika*
the Buffalo Soldiers scratch with soap
on concrete walls

        of this prison—
        a private enterprise
        sponsored by Liberty Wheat—

            and separate but equal
            glass coins
            of the realm—

Welcome to Lockdown Amerika
where Bigger says

           White can't be made right without

Black as a newfangled Brotherhood
of Don't Ask Don't Tell
Foreclosures Occupied   Iron Rings in Yellow Wallpapered Walls

Machinists Inside the Machine Inside the Machinery

The guard promises your children on the outside don't need you
The guard says c'mon, children are resilient
The guard marvels that children have their own stockades!
                       with earth for pillows!
                       with sky for blankets!
                       with ragweed for food!

The guard avows that when Martin and Malcolm and Presidents
are assassinated
        there are safety plans in place

      for the children
      to duck and cover
                           —according
                           to NRA Protocols!—

    inside large pumpkins
    carved with exceptionalism
    and naturally insulated   with asbestos fiber
                                 beneath a coating
                                 of mercury

but understandably a child
or two or————————————————————————————
must be sacrificed   for the Common Good
                         and the Common Goods

    since everyone
    has weapons———— all quick-smooth
                     Winchester 1892s!

————The guard says that for their own benefit,
    the children must be tested:
            a. acid rain
            b. acid air
            c. acid soil
            d. acid sea

                Yes, the children must be tested————

He loves drug laws!
He spreads welcome hugs!

We're a family, you see.

> Enjoy the rotational gravy the rotational grazing—
> It's a Certified Animal Feeding Operation!

Ah!

highcalorieherbicidesantibioticshormonesvitamins!

increasedyieldsoffiberandfoodperacre!

thresherstractorscombinesplanterstransplanters!

> Hot, fresh Common Wheat
> bread, so blonde, so soft, every morning—
> for free!

You'll be debeaked to decrease harm from fighting.
No need for concern—it's painless
and ultimately beneficial. You'll see—
as time passes, you'll be grateful
to enjoy the—.

I see a raised hand out there! Not to worry,
we like hoodies here
and have a crack team
that resews
them as straightjackets
with complimentary
leg irons.

Just be sure not
to light smokes
in the methane plume
or, heh, our Friendly Fracosaurus
might shale you behind
the counterinsurgency.

Another one! Sure, I know
those posters

in your cells
of manacled
Glyphosate Glen-Glinda
are hot—try not
to pledge
allegiance—
it's drill and chill, folks,
just chill and drill.

Any more questions? Oh, don't worry about shitting
in the lagoon—it all goes
downstream
where we later harvest
the zinccopperchromiumarseniccadmiumlead
after it's dried
by enemy combatants.

And not to fret 'bout that slipping
coal ash slush
pond: our chemicals
are proprietary, so rest assured,
they are consumable
and of the finest
quality.

Active shooters? Collateral
Damage? Blessedly
we've been trained
to lock our rifles
into lockdown—plus
Texting and Twittering and Facebooking
make sure we are all
safe.

The future? When you graduate
there are transitional
FBI-CIA Monoculture Motels
for immigrants
and miscreants

who slowly acquire valuable
life skills as Keystone XL
donut factory
team members
and learn

our equation that   Deaths of Sand

                                              =

                              A Birth of Glass

tailings at *La Linea*, The Boundary, where Coywolf
stops Little Red Riding Hood and asks, "Where are
you headed? What are you carrying?"

————

"I'm off to my abuela's house," says Little Red Riding
Hood. "I'm bringing her pico and nopalitos."

————

"You must choose," says Coywolf, pointing to two
paths, fenced, of sharpened glass shards:
          Needles   or   *Pins*

————

"Which path do you prefer?" Coywolf asks. "The Path
of Crystal Needles or the Path of Crystal Pins?"

————

"I'll take the Path of Crystal Pins," says the girl.

————

"Well done!" Coywolf replies. "I'll take the Path of
Crystal Needles, and we'll see who gets there first!"

————soon Coywolf and Little Red Riding Hood arrive,
          paws
          and feet pricked
          into gore,

not at Ellis Island,
but

at a plastic
rose-twined scapular
of the Virgin

melted by desert
sun and baked
into a dead

woman's breasts . . . .

her shoes missing
her toe tips black

with bruises
like periods
at air's end

her heart exploded   from cocaine
given   to make her walk

faster
across Coahuila . . . .

fleeing a village
that had lost
its men——

                (to a Houston stash house
                of 100 husbandsfathersbrotherssons
                ear-to-ear in 1,000 square feet)

to America——

——its eagle perched
on blooming prickly pear
a still live snake
between its talons———

              ———The Aztecs called poetry *xochitl in cuicatl*
                        "the flower and the song"—
            There were only three genres of lyric, divided by topic:
        war   creation   flowers——

——So Warcreationflowers

questions,   *The trouble*
                  With this America

Is that we birthed it
But did not make it?
Or that we did not birth it
But made it—————?

And make it—————?

—————into jealous dressing
in Marlboros,
suspicions of Budweiser?

A vision that someone else, not us,
might be the superior sun?
ProChoice/ProLife?
Glyphosate/Gluphosinate?
Castro/Kennedy?
Monsanto/Organic?
Roosevelt/Stalin?

Because they have moremoremore?

The gods:
Didn't you know
that any stone, even a pebble,
will someday
exchange you for the moss
of time——
of history——

>——*of mettā*

——*of merge*————<

—————into this Heart Mountain Relocation Center, 1943—
sanded butte light, your husband interned/drafted/
now dead for the crime
of being Japanese—evenings

you pluck melancholy airs on kotos, break rice
cakes, scorch government books
in the hibachi to savor
smoke, consider life

as a Buddhist nun—and you learn
    Chinese just to be
    perverse, embellishing all with scenes of brushed
    ink on scarce paper, so that words

erase self erases just black gardens and ponds
    remain, skimming like plum blossoms
    on streams before your Japanese-Czech granddaughter
    reading them three decades later—

she is > skin-to-skin soul-to-soul <
    close to you, future~floating
    in her walk-up above Avenue D———

———while below, gummy
pay phone cord left swinging,

> you are another young woman: <

Boston Brahmin, smack
pale, sauntering,

silver-blue mink stole, cat
eyes stretched heavenward

with kohl, back to where your son,
father, and car idle until the boy play-snaps

the brake free, and your father, never
having driven, grabs shift

from chauffeur and mistakenly
lurches the car into reverse, crushing you shrieking,

stumbling backward and falling,
seeing only the underbelly of a rusting

Chevy, Speed Lube, Car Wash
Special $2.95,

> before slowly drifting soulborne <

past a lone sycamore—and a streetlight sign
that says, *Clearance: 10 Feet*

Hung one block from
The Hell's Angels annual Fourth of July block party
Where a gunpowder sack, stuffed in a trash can,
Receives a flame kiss, and Pepsi/Miller bottles smash
Into flying knives: a shard pierces your throat,
You this watching boy, fourteen, at that instant
Pondering the crumpled metal bin, the waste
Of what could have been
A container for rice, jute, or glassfishes
In your Bangladesh—and your blood
Whorls like Islamic temple
Mosaics transforming doors' blank
Frames into ambiguous filigree,
Marking the ever morphing border
Between bottle glass and dagger,
Between young man and still heart,
Inscribing the lack
Of dichroic language
For your self-soul in exit——

or for placenta
            slipping away   wasp
                        subtracting stinger   tear
                                    loosening——<

——Best to drift~sift then, *loose*, no Berlin Wall barriers but breeze

                    |because borderwalls grow|

[Iwo Jima: 1945]   *[Fallujah: 2004]*
lives in Suribachi foxholes,   woes between
drama of rust. To move   Abu Ghraib
is a shore, each moment   and vibrato. Sand can't
an engine   argue as bombs cleave

of difference. Straddle
trench latrines, whore baths
from water-filled
helmets. Even rocks

charge. Moldy bully beef,
hardtack, and above smoke
slowly weds. When might
checkmate
relax? The colonel

of dusk in his tie
of burnt soldiers,
slipping
astronomies. Now fate
unbuttons as the Night

Police fire, lakes
of summer dying.
Wounds like mud,
we savages
of carbon. *If you get a flag*

to the top, put it up. I will plant
caramel islands, the paleskin teen
marine says—patch
beard aquiver
as blood lungfills
from shrapnel—

and mountains with jelly toast
summits. His childhood
replies: To shake

is mulch smell
and bright fall leaves

the garage! IEDs,
RPGs, white
phosphorus shake
'n bake. Breath

waits, ever patient
between desert clouds
and all clocks. Thermos
full of hard candy.
On the asphalt,

lanes scatter. To drift,
the major shouts,
is nothing
but fucking.
All cottages—

picket clutched,
roseate—
then become legend.
Fedayeen
and running from

sullen flack. We swab
our raw crotches
with salicylic acid
because no patrol
reflects. These generals
are lawyers for fungus,

our dead beaten
and then set
ablaze. Even the fabric

of sea elides into wrath,
not float. Hear those

against gusts. Then
the milk foxes

and feathers, this lull
white sepulcher
of swinging snow———

leaving

our broken of war
paraquadri plegics | and the mindgones | soulgones

not swinging————→

leaving only

American three *G*s, not three *R*s:

        holy trinity trinitite sheaf
        of
        God   Guns   Gridiron

        not Trikāya
        of
        Dharmakāya   **S**ambhogakāya   **N**irmānakāya

leaving only

our CTE   NFL
football   linemenrunningbackswidereceiversguards

not swinging————

————granted, like shorn dragon
flies dipped
in egg
white, blown
with high fructose
sanding sugar——

those boys can stiffen, crystal-spangled,
and sue,
but would not be whole————————————

screams as they burn
within tanks? Blackened,

U.S. Army contractors
aswing, lynched from bridges
above this Euphrates———

ANTIDOTE

I was born in a wheat field snapping my fingers.

—Tomaž Šalamun, "The Tree of Life"

. . . The gods
we played with broke, they were made of glass.

—Dean Young, "My People"

For you, forsythia. The
grass in my glass.

—Lyn Hejinian, *My Life*

─────────────────────can stiffen, yes, but not be whole───

──because wholeness is
for this paraquadri

plegic to make love—
each inner elbow becoming

a vulva, his/her
honey soles) honey palms)

honey tree. Catheter dew
tipped. For this mer
maid suck
ling pig, lap washed

with balsam & plunder, horned
crown. Each paraquadri

is the fist
my womb loves best so   sO   ∧   sO   ∧   sO

    Let's bring the placing of the cotton,
    homespun, upon black Harney silt loam ~~

    Let's bring the limned grains
    of the microbe-pink Salt Lake ~~

    Let's bring the Dakota white bison
    and its holy yoke ~~

    Let's bring the bellflower
    and long-tongued bees of the *me* ~~

    Let's bring the Wisconsin buttercake, the bare golden
    maid on the dripping McIntosh apple ~~

    Let's bring the undersouls of early,
    tall-stemmed Boulder morels ~~

Let's bring the protea of women
and the dildo of auroral ~~

Let's bring the duduk, the erhu, the banjo,
and the cowrie tambourines.

Yet after, we all push
To Grenada's ossuary,
Tongues parsnipped

With the chill,
Bittering gorse of bloating
Trespasses. Tripping

On hybrid pumpkins, ensnared
In Gore-Tex vines, rising
Only to fall again and again

On U.S. glass—
Each failure and descent
Barbing our spirits,

As we cannot
Become clean of

Those who paint sharp pilgrims over the city.
Those who break flowers and Manhattan towers.
Those who appear like plastic carnations up close.
Those who mail ruins and anthrax.
Those who quiver with greed as if kissing.
Those who hunt Amish schoolgirls.
Those who pat heaving levees.

Those who survive the rigors of love.

Oh Wrestling Jacob, here comes the dawn!
I've still got you . . . .

You see, some devoted gardeners, singing
Arbeit Macht Frei,

fed human char to Nazi gardens
of vegetable   and rose————

                              thirteen million murdered
                              JewsRomaHomosexuals
                              PoliticalPrisonersWarPrisoners
                              Jehovah'sWitnesses————

————so our antidote
is that the responsible void
                    of the Homeland Father

is *not* our doctrine————

                    then at last   I can lift   your openwork
                         veil   but to stare
                    does overwhelm joy

                    you agree   of course weapons
                                                 should grieve

                                                 for the children—

                                                 and yes
                                                 all souls crave

                                                 erotic bedrock—

          merely to arrive, you add, is sex

———

however I fear
your wisdom
and fail   to reveal
     that one ginger nipple
is double
the other

yet arrives your redeem:
that ritual of palm   fingertips   lime prosthetic
                    and thumb   and tongue
muslin wrapping   my tall scaffolds
of twistiron

later, our pillow
embroidery reads:
Why Are We Dying?

———

our flesh   becomes glass   our arms
lightning reeds   not bent   in Others' wind

our unknown   thickets forth
from our streams' long sky   of futurity

gilding we tread
        above
        chemical   dregs

        above
        oceans
        of snowmelt

        above
        GMO berries

        above
        fungal monarchs
        speared   on briars   of the Holocene

———

in time my hindmilk   fills your valentines
of postwar parch

our wetting   testimony
of the sea   and carbon

so: you let me mate
                     your dragon

I birth   100 eggs—
we raise each babe   for 7,000 years

teach them
        how to be married

where   to find salt

———
with age
our satisfaction   spreads lovely—
                                chaos undone—

forever lost   our jowls   of decorum

no mission   resisting   our world
            of coupling—

———

at last   our sacrificial bowls   pure   recall
                                how to dance
then rain becomes a wheel
and powder? a kiss

so that is love, dears: our alcove
                      warm   crowded
and openmouthed
in the figment house———

transparent ~ our circular ascent———
            O ring within ring within ring O

forgetting smokestacks
to savor   passengers   of grass———

like the toddler who says———

                ———My fur is green. No one is the master
                of sand, but to walk is beginning. Early strides
                deserve a brass band. Oolong voice
                of Mother Eve, her breast clamped
                in my plump beak. This summer, the sliding
                maples are warm sandals
                of weather, and the insects,
                always underdressed, popsicle revel———

———thus cheered, you'll loafe with me again now . . . . among our sheaves . . . .
a shattering . . . . a chiming . . . .

How we rest now in December

atop our postbellum globeshards
and splinters

your tongue plunges   ~   to my gristled heart

and reaches   ~   till you stop my little wounds
and reaches   ~   till you shod my feet
and reaches   ~   beyond shiver

to silence   <

observe! my knife shavings of flesh
and soul healed!
breastfed fields of colostrum bloom

each grain safely softstarch
beneath stiff   beeswing
epidermis——

——more life below
        ground than above   so we star-nosed moles
        wiggle our celestial   Egyptian wheat grain
        as part of us   and of the darkness——

White Tārā tau
∞ eyes opening in the forehead
&palms&soles

no male ——— no female
no American ——— no Other
no ocean
of existence = suffering

thus we exalt   inter   ~   national

> sprung~joined from glass tears
on the faces   of our Gods
of the Worlds ←——

————and so we must love
with sacrifice

to the dove   of America's day in this world:

Sequoia queens sprouting ~~
~~ endlessly ~~ from their boles ~~

~~ a pipevine swallowtail tasting ~~
~~ through its feet ~~

~~ a female opossum with two vaginas ~~
~~ two cervixes ~~ two uteri ~~ carrying yolk sacs ~~

~~ each housefly always ~~ humming ~~
~~ in the perfect key ~~ of *F* ~~

~~ the molting tarantula ~~ replacing ~~ internal organs ~~
~~ genitalia ~~ and lost limbs ~~

~~ the nursery web spider ~~
~~ clamping fangs ~~ to lift silken eggs ~~

~~ today ~~ like Costa's hummingbird ~~
~~ we eat twice our weight ~~

~~ in penstemon nectar ~~
~~ strip and cloak ~~ with Savannah graybeards ~~

~~ of Spanish moss ~~ the brittle frillery ~~
~~ and clasp ~~ a female leatherback turtle ~~

~~ diving 4,000 feet ~~ on one breath ~~
~~ then deeper still ~~ jade darkness ~~

~~ at last north ~~ through blue whale ~~
~~ blood vessels ~~ large enough for any person ~~

~~ to trespass ~~

The bare of them—of their nature—
And of our nakedness————————a herald, a gift!

Our groom of *ah's* straining
in the western holster,
our second life of southern dreams

walking the sky

to Pollock   of the east, so strummed
by stream ~ flex

that he doesn't bother   to mix—
or even
to use   a brush——

> Yep, at the deepest level of Bang : Crunch,
we are one United

                                        Plumb

                Subcutaneous   Thrum⟵——

——except for our California *More,*
a sham salad:

acres of shrouded gourmet herb
imidaclopridDCPADimethomorph lettuce,
· · · — — · ·

hothouse *FlavrSavr* tomatoes too much stuffed
with campylobactersalmonellafactoryshredchicken
· · · — — · · ·

                limp dill

and ethylenediaminetetraacetic acid mayonnaise
· · · — — · · ·

dessert desert of ethyl acetate pineapple gelati   melting
· · · — — · · ·

and on the table, plastic
OIL   images of   wee brown Hawai'ian pineapple
                                  wheat stalks dried
                                  bluebells
                                  grapes Chile black & New York amber

CLOTH   trim red gingham

. . . _ _ _ . . .

<

But *my more*
is footplay, saloon breasts—
O you tender Pioneers of Globe,
Here's my safe cradle!

<

Owl-eyed
are my wounds: the Ladies
yumstop them
like pomegranates

(although I, too, have a Wife
among the masonry)

<

Thus my script,
scrawled:
let bare be the gleaming slick thighs
of fire engines—

my spring elk splendor—
wet this hymn my trunk your leaves——

——Ladies, those who hunt must now leave my meadow

——The rest may remain, agape, in my newborn
                        Country————

————————because now it is **I** it is **I** it is **I**,

                              Eve!

                        age 16, 1929——
                              ordering,

        Quick, get giggle juice and rinse me pretty. I'm gonna have an
        ing-bing. Right here! Right now!

Ain't that the clam's garter. Bankers divin' from buildings? I'm
on the nut, too, but you don't see me dressin' in no

wood kimono. It's all a clip joint. Pass me your deck o' luckies.
No? Go climb up your thumb. Aw, don't put the screws

on, you big palooka. I skate around plenty. Here's a sawbuck for
tiger milk. Hotsy

totsy, and how! Ain't that the flea's eyebrows. Here comes my
player. Don't take a powder, Sam: I've got gams

on ice. Sure them bankers fell, but we're still spiffy. Like my
skin of caramel? So then

where's my meat, Daddy-O? I'm a bearcat with bubs, a moll o'
mazooza. But get there fast, and you get there solo. Woof, woof,

chippy. Slow burn, skidoo, you're on My trolley——

——————because now it is **I** it is **I** it is **I**,

Lucy and the Parsons
of Anarchy——

proclaiming,

When the prison, stake or scaffold
can no longer silence the voice
of the protesting minority, progress
moves on a step, but not until then——

for
we are the slaves of slaves never be deceived that
the rich will allow you to vote away their
wealth let us sink such differences as nationality,
religion, politics anarchism has but one infallible,
unchangeable motto, "freedom" to discover any
truth, freedom to develop, to live naturally and
fully you are not absolutely defenseless for the
torch of the incendiary, which has been known
with impunity, cannot be wrested from you the

*unjust institutions which work so much misery
and suffering to the masses have their root in
governments, and owe their whole existence to
the power derived from government we cannot
help but believe that were every law, every title
deed, every court, and every police officer or
soldier abolished tomorrow with one sweep, we
would be better off than now*

*Oh, Misery, I have drunk thy cup of sorrow to
its dregs, but I am still a rebel**——

————————and so am **I** so am **I** so am **I**,

       Ida of Wells, Wells of Ida——

           proclaiming,

*I will not begin at this late day by doing what
my soul abhors;*

sugaring men . . . with flattery——

——decades before Rosa,
Ida refusing to move   to the smoking car——
conductor   and two men   dragging her
refusing suing refusing suing refusing suing refusing suing

teachereditornewspaperownerinvestigativejournalistsuffragist

mother

Ida protesting publishing protesting publishing protesting
boycotting the 1893 World's Fair for snubbing blacks

      hear ye her *Southern Horrors*——
lynched for opening a grocery store
        across the street from a white grocery store

---

* All italicized phrases in the "Lucy and the Parsons of Anarchy" section are the words of
Lucy Gonzalez Parsons, and the two italicized quotations in the "Ida of Wells, Wells of Ida"
section were written by Ida B. Wells.

lynched for being in debt
lynched for refusing to move
lynched for being drunk——

   ——save our money and leave a town
    which will neither protect our lives and property,

    nor give us a fair trial in the courts,
    but takes us out and murders us——

       ——Ida leaving

   America

    by dying while writing
    her autobiography—

  in mid-sentence   in mid-word——

——her America also
  always in mid-sentence   *in mid-word——*

because

35,000 walruses   beach   on sand after failing
     to find   home   platforms of ice

weekly   the girl polishes   every Winchester model
    made from 1892 to 1982   until her cheeks   pinken

the remains of a star can fit   in a matchbox
    yet weigh   40 billion   tons

bangs flipping   like a hula skirt   the Akron teenager
    rides her dealer   teacher   in a hammock

oak trees   cannot make acorns   until age fifty

lonely bachelor   deaf   raises flamingoes in the basement

Help me I don't want to be here   cries   the kindergartener
   Well you're here   says a gray   young man   then shoots

bald eagle feathers   weigh more   than their skeletons

Mike the headless   chicken survives 18 months
    on eyedropper milk   and mashed corn

Chinese–American physicist   cools atoms
      then moves them   like toys

unable   to evacuate   she stays crouched   cinder-block hallway
     hurricane trees   cracking   shelter dogs   whinehowl

leg muscles   of a locust   are one thousand
    times stronger   than ours

the miscarried   are discarded   as medical waste

after scrubbing   the gristmill   children hide
    watermelons   in Maine haystacks   for winter

the bois all relish
    how her fingers   tremble   like pulses
                          on their lips

male and female   anglerfish   attach
    forever no release   their veins   unite

dust bowl farmer   lactates and feeds
    his infant daughter   wife tubercular
             chocolate brown   sputum

Missoula pimp   slaps cologne on neck
    adjusts collar   daisyskull ring raps on semi cab
        to offer   the boy

father pulls   plastic trash bags   from pantry
    to gather   his son's body   pieces   Oklahoma
    bomb site

my doubles are a jaguar   she says   lacing
    black vinyl chaps   *and a sacrificial knife*

to detect bats   night butterflies   have ears
     on their wings

after stabbing   his mother   the wan   Telegraph Avenue
    chef   prepares   tarte tartin   green
      beans amandine   trout   on a rhubarb leaf

San Francisco 1906   earthquake   a crater city
    20,000 camped   around El Presidio Real   burning

Piano Red shouts   while slamming   barrelhouse blues

each AIBO   robot   has five basic instincts
    searchmoverechargelovesleep

the animal   whose teeth   most closely
    resemble ours   is the pig

at brunch   the teen celebrates   painless abortion
    of fetus stewed   in frat party   Rohypnol punch

lost bones   shift and pile   deep-sea wreck
    Montauk

granmama tells   grandson   of police dogs   chewing off
    fingers   KKK flogging   Selma
        as he helps   pick peas and clean catfish

one   bristlecone pine   White Mountains
    more than 4,800 years   on earth

drag queen   named Heart of Dixie   adorned
    in doilies   Chanel slingbacks
        earrings   of gilded   Carolina tobacco

to make love   she carries him   from wheelchair
    to sofa   to floor   to armchair

breasts leaking   enlarging bones   she buries
    the baby   empty lot   before light

beneath ocean   striped sea robins   Atlantic croakers
    talk and sing

Senator   stuffs another   fingerling potato
    in his   blue thong   behind a Castro bar

cow alive with no hide   twigs like spears   in her neck   Jarrell F5

Alabama nuclear plant   shut down   Tennessee River water
    too warm   for reactor   cooling

father pushes   aside wires   weeps and cups   premature daughter
    eyelids crimpedbruised   she kitten yelps

high school boy   opens 50 capsules   into soupy
    ice cream   stirs and sips
            forever sleeps curled   in the garden shed

Ohio father   of six   ten prison years   Louisiana hard labor
    for two joints   in hip pocket

icebow   Barrow Alaska
    then the sun sets   for 65 days

artists painted raiding miners   bound   "Indians" pouring
    molten gold   in o-horror mouths

dog named Bud   wearing goggles   drives
    across America   in 1903

mother pinches   skinfold on child's ivory stomach
    slides   insulin needle in   child
              continues   tapping PDA

after torpedoes   Ensign   in fire pajamas runs   from ship bunk
    to deck   of USS *California*   dies   with burned
        claw hands   reaching   for ocean

each group   of jellyfish   no matter how lethal
    is called   a *bloom*

Nuyorican   firefighter watches   best friend   crushed
    mid-smile   by Twin Tower   falling man

girl sleeps   on her stomach Beverly Hills cabana
    stepfather bite marks   raw across
           her back

half the geysers   on earth   are in Yellowstone

waxlike grandfather   rocks on porch
    after grandson's funeral   single red rose   in peach
       crewelwork bassinet

Plymouth Colony   reenactor   albino   hides sunscreen
     and e-reader   inside   a copper kettle

wife finds   ice cream in dryer   socks on mug shelf
    Alzheimer's husband   forgets
       their five-year-old son   at the park

ritual whale kill   same day   *maktak* is flown
    to Inupiat aunts   in Wichita

liquid   within young coconuts
    is a replacement   for human   plasma

the lemon   contains   more sugar than the orange——

——so after establishing a supernatural environment within he levitates hard into my perineum taste of malt and over our heads the plasmic seas close up forgiving that this woman seems beautiful if seen from behind but is not when viewed from the front and refuses

like a camel to produce milk until her nostrils have been tickled ah jism I must strive to disremember those ancient Greeks who forced

gal(ley) slaves to wear metal collars while grinding wheat so that they could not eat it the iron inscribed in Latin *I have run away/Catch me/Reward* now freed they all help me to fill the cannon

chargers with powder ram rags then pack in the steel balls where *women walk*—no, *a woman walks* into a New Bedford bar and is raped atop a pool table by six men

while twenty men watch later she is caged for ten decades in a suburban basement dungeon sure it's better to shed history and

grammar those saboteurs of wonder *more
dangerous than the strategic deferral of choice is
the romance of conviction* so be my

meme dollface in this glass house and over
our heads the seas' sweet fever shields us
from falling rifles

falling factory farm fracking despots
merry—

——yes, merry marry me, swain or maid or——

if we shit a golden egg
let's be lucky not prudish—
catch it in a pretty cup——

——for my duchess, my darling
like the sun uncorked, chainless snow——

So now we brown dream girls marry
in mountain air. Asters kneel,

nodding. How did we lose a life
together of damp nocturnes, tropic

homes steaming? Restart—but let's deep
walk this time. Come certain!

Sure now! Stoop not—and run back
to our love-torn stockings. Let's *pas de chat*

with our soft coffee
flesh. Glissade without clothes. My sweet,

our glass bead necklaces are green
and tiny bright leaders,

unstrung. At last we'll meet All. Together.
Thrones blown, multiple darks. Horizons

of shiver? *Pour*——

——because after the wintry diagnosis
   that my lungs will be soon-blue
from asbestos,
   we still can flame
   the ether—
my blood loud and glued,
winds sinking—
our hands in grief becoming serpent-footed fish,
clasped together —despite rising floe
    —despite no restraining
the sudden wide poison
in my flesh captive
to paths unsprung—and yet—
happy denial, like surface,
still dolphins this region—

so as if from sea we upfloat, sidelong—
pregnant in and by lakes,
palm to palm, pretending
we are fluid undefiled—
so that we can
meet lightness—and not shatter,

but *Run*——

   ——back to morning orchid cakes come sprawling.
  Tropicana congas on scarlet butter, warm plantains,
  pastelitos. Our dresses become pillows, smoke and sunder.
  In Jersey we were housewives, barnacled. No longer.
  Without husbands, princes, kings, our night bracelets are
  now steamed

  through. Her rings of breasts
  and mine enlarge with dears,

  no edges, queering. Sugared café au lait, cigars. Shea makes
  our afros glisten. Our flanges of love heat gleaming. And
  Cyril's at the Sans Souci, jazzing

reason! Mariposa, shutters, foxtrot, her russet thighs,
moon. My love, she is split guava, cocoa croqueta. Our
teacups bliss past, rowing——<

——to those discernible coonskin caps that are

Q   tongues studded
                with cloves
    and sequins   cured
       in myrrh   raccoons
swinging from the belfry
        béchamel
        on rye
this morning
           your left wrist
       lisps
          my patchouli   unclasp !
                  thighs   fill
           me dear not
                         to mention
                       the gods

Q   after daubing
             aureoles violet
  jimmy
    some henna
  doodle
lactiferous   mammals
           on each calf
    slick after
        garam
masala   Petrarch
        wore   a snood
  nay a caul
    of birch bark   (and lime rinds!)
        well forgive
         for I'm built
    like a gooseneck
                 faucet

Q   balls gilded
          bergamot
         refrescos   I'm your ramada
      all mouths   overgrown
but welcome
           great dane   doubloon   pluck
         the lemons   from my
navel   the seaside
           life!   for a time   aloft
      on whale
        spume   palazzo ah
                    for shame   I thought
                        your name
                            was
                      not   ralph

Q   tear into the withers
     of your roma
         tomato   salted   wrapped
argyle   piano upload
      future storms and radar
            sweeping!
        away guano
               how many times
               for the assignation   girl?

Q   powdered capstone
     of his mage
tower   making
     couch love
       while dachshunds
watch   each tit has its own
        microclimate   huichol
        veins   strumming
      the plexiglas   window
        on my chest   you can look
              but don't tap!
        so as not   to scare
                    the fish

Q   raisin   in the outfield   i'm not especially
                    humongous
        toothy   gnu cheekbones   at night
                    the mice
deign   to enter   in tiny leather
                            masks   he bends
            over me   weeping!   willow
                depart
        buster   my hip flask contains
                    the ganges   wag
            out   of my glade
                                                theater
            time   to go
                    hungry   live and love
                        in tunnels beneath
                                        the autobahn

Q   winged the oranges
                complacencies
            of the pain   noir   raw
                                        steak

                    to each breast
        at the Red Scoot
        Inn   satisfaction
                of big boots   and silk bra pushup
                    few know
my fretwork   bleed
                    the water   clear

            jehovah!
        punched   brass pineapple

                            make
                                me property
                                of the year

                    .   .   .

Q   your phallus   bears
                                squid-like
appendages
            inspired
                        by Shakespeare
happy toad
                        in tweeds   I spread
        my orient   beams
see?   we both   are bent
        in our undergrowth   waiters
                        of the world
        all pregnant!
                like the moon   pop
        it   your charm
                        can make   one heap
                                                of all our beings

Q   we only   come round
            once
        each century   pied
            the ectoplasmic
penis bobs
            in colorado
                streams Mister
                                Lovely   my center
            is space
            not mass   snake
drum   never
    full repast   burn
            forsooth!   cinder
                        yeah but I
                        still   have cookies
                                        to give
                                                too

Q   her spine
         a flip-flop   hair
             copper wire   fetch
       me atomic   dog
           then please   admit
we're still   on the vine   cervical
                  pudding   sleep
    walking   with a strut   twitch!
      you fear   i'm your future
     home   cowgirl?
        just   at the apple edges
                           of your mind

Q   on bad days   I wear
       bonnet
              and catheter
                      infidel
kibitz   the stormy petrel
    if we all   stiffen
      the soft   excrete   holy?
          ex voto
    your leftover   semen   like lucite
          on the headboard
    pork bun   luncheon
redemption   mercy ain't   always
      forgiveness   aw heck
    kiss!
        my buttercup   cook
            while I strip   looking

                  ·   ·   ·

Q   put   my earrings

in an old nest

of sparrows   following

a night   of lovemaking   no surprise

when your tongue   protrudes

from my navel

grand   solar man—

meeting a weasel

is ominous

encountering   a hog

pernicious—

mmm but   mating   a gorilla

is beneficial

as he makes   speechless!   the one

who sees

him   first

Q   please open   me and insert

your dioramas   so

we enter   the long   house

berries

falling   from the ceiling   the finale

although crowded   is lonely

placental

rivets   thrown wide

the door   into birdness

seraphim

give the lowdown   yet

on tricycles   foment?

you ask   blowing

trumpets   through   my hair

yup   stabbed through!

we're closer

to truth

Q   fountains
         of wade   salmon
           salvation   bikini car wash
           not just   for truckers wanting
        to forget   femme fur   shamrock
i'm a one-way
        noodle   morph
      this old horse into   a sweet shoppe
        dogwood
           in my crevices
     tam   bourine!
      vanilla rubbed   mons—
                   transport
                   is a covenant——

——*yes, transport*
       is a covenant——

——that can even heal

an indwelling within the body's HIV
drawers of polar—hospital walls
like tallow. Even touching
pleasures are wretched? Chest
a lethargic shelf? Surely something enwraps
this cock
of dust?

whichloverwhichloverwhichloverwhichloverwhichloverwhichloverwhich

Please gift me back The Regular Country. Here fluorescent

noon burns all pills, sears all love and nooks. Kaposi's gums, CD4
count falling. Skies have become
plague horsemen—so let's vet
the spirits and make them
accountable.

whichloverwhichloverwhichloverwhichloverwhichloverwhichloverwhich

Like tresses, our kind marriage tropics
my sleep, prompting
some HAART god to wither the stings. Then from these wounds
a blazing is heard, and in their wood
streams a temple where deer like us, water bearded,
can still lichen rest.

whichloverwhichloverwhichloverwhichloverwhichloverwhichloverwhich

Together, our burgeon heart splices me
the laurel of our child, embracing. Robin surprise,
and a revisit to the sheen
fleets of East. Skin flakes kiss, stitch
together, and the white pox
smooths into glow.

whichloverwhichloverwhichloverwhichloverwhichloverwhichloverwhich

Please don't remind me about who
has vanished into The Off. Remember: I once bit
pears after making love on the spring
shed roof, our tool belts wallets work
boots tumbling? Remember: *The rocks I flower*——
and *flower I the rocks*——

——to balm another sickness
that is, according to Amerika, a crime——

       ——for which they are arrested and then loaded at gun-
      point into a ship's cattle stalls. Upon sight of Moloka'i's
      tuff peaks, each man is thrown overboard with one
      khaki woolen blanket, shards of salt beef, and a shovel or
      axe. Women receive a blanket and nothing else. Smashed
      by waves

      ashore, they find two clapboard cottages with seawind

      hissing slats. On nothing they live but the corned
      meat—then pond apples—then insects. Water caught in
      date palm fronds. In time, they wheedle taro-sweet

potatoes-onions-guava to grow in old ashfall. Sugarcane moonshine, jump-started with spit, drunk more than water—especially when blindness sets in for some. Afternoon sweet narcotic dreams from awa roots, pulped then

strained. Nightly soon daily brawls and madness un-hemmed by the 3,000-foot-high cliff pen, so steep that wild goats plummet to death—and are promptly roasted, devoured whole, even hooves soaked and sucked. *Feet my fingers,* says one man again and again, all but one thumb lost to infection and numb. *Feet*

my fingers. Sometimes they slaughter a squat black pig fattened on sweet potato vines—or share poi like family. Overseers and years cause more shacks to be built, even churches even a clinic. The new surgeon knows that when deep cuts are made to skin, the Hansen's body retracts and widens, deepening the hole to be

stitched. During evenings, that doctor, imported from Mexico, fingers her rosary and reads old medical texts and treatises on bush medicine. While eating corn tortillas, she learns: If short of wheat, medieval cooks made wound-like open pies called traps—closed ones were called *coffyns,* or coffins. She learns: Wounds are still sealed, in some parts of South America, by application of scarab beetles. (As they eat along both cut edges, their necks are held and twisted,

leaving heads stiff and stuck tight, binding the gap like staples.) She learns: The recipe for a drawing salve of lobelia and goldenseal, which should be tamped in the wound and then stitched

closed with long needles.

On the island
there is no goldenseal
or lobelia.

There are no long needles.

Every afternoon a boy walks past the doctor's clinic window, going home from the missionary's school and chanting Mele Kahuli, *Chant of the Tree-Shell*—

Kahuli aku,	*Trill a-far,*
Kahuli mai,	*Trill a-near,*

Kahuli lei ula,	*A dainty song-wreath,*
Lei akolea.	*Wreath akolea.*

Kolea, kolea,	*Kolea, kolea,*
Ki'i ka wai,	*Fetch me some dew,*
Wai akolea.	*Dew from pink akolea.*

Then he plays ulu maika, rolls finger-shaped rocks beneath the gum-myrtle

trees. At lunch the doctor makes primitive sketches of her favorite birds, rust-brown 'elepaios who cry

"oh no! oh no!" One evening she secretly watches the boy's mother hand-feed him guava, breadfruit, banana, poi. *He must feel loved,* she thinks, *to get strong.* Scars from the doctor's biopsy cuts will become bogs in the boy— and he will eventually lose

each ear to infection. After hearing the mother plans to flee to the jungle with her son, the doctor fills all her blankets—eight total—with dried fish and fruit, gourds, nets, arrows, knives, axes, bullets, and gunpowder stolen from supply barrels—then ties them with vines to create knapsacks—

> *Dear Jesus, do something—*

and leaves them secretly
before her door in the night

> *Dear Jesus, do something—*

while in her dreams

the boy's mother speaks
with Queen Liliʻuokalani, who whispers—

I see no protection
if you stayed—

      At first I trusted   *America*
      boat after boat
      —their Marines—their plantations—

      yet the U.S. of A. so-called judge
      called to pass sentence on me

      had stone
      after stone
      rain

      from his glass house = glass mouth——

      ——because the All   *he wanted*   *they wanted*

          was sandalwood+sugar+pineapple
          and moremoremore——

——yes, the sacred taro   *our kalo*   *once voted,*
  and voted well——

——its   *ha*   *breath*   *like a stem*
  and   *piko*   *navel*   *where stem meets leaf*
  the   *keiki*   *children*   *shoots around mother plant*
  Hawaiʻi   *one*   *ʻohana*   *kalo*   *family——*

          But into that closeness entered the American intruders.
              Their new spartan official ration   *of leis.*

    Their "United" Constitution
    Made of Funds?

    Doling of Dole.

    Lava those   *Marines*
    who freely mobbed

    my name.

O, I UNDERSTAND EXTREMELY NOW Mr. J. S. Walker came and told me "that he ha
d come on a painful duty, that the opposition party had requested that I should abdicate." I told him
that I had no idea of doing so, but that I would like to see Mr. Neumann. Half an hour later he returned

THEIR FALSE LIKEYOULIKEME

with that gentleman, and I explained to him my positi *TREATY.*

THOSE US/U.S. STRANGERS CHANTED TRICKERY on, and he advised that I should consult my

friends. I immediately sent for Messrs. J. O. Carter, Damon, Widemann, Cleghorn, my mi *THAT SPREAD.*
nisters; Messrs. Neumann, Walker, and Macfarlane also being present. The situation being taken into consideration, it was found th
at, since the troops of the United States had been landed to support the revolutionists, by the orde   the American minister, it
would be impossible for us to make any resistance. Mr. Damon had previously intimated to Mr. P   it was useless to resis
t, their party was supported by the American minister. Mr. Damon also said   meetin   understood that I shou

FIRED. ld remain at the palace, and continue to fly the royal standard. At six P.M. I signed   I, Liliuokalani,
by the grace of God and under the constitution of the Hawaiian kingdom Queen, do hereby sol   ny and all acts
done against myself and the constitutional government of the Hawaiian kingdom by certain persons   established a Pr
ovisional Government of and for this kingdom. That I yield to the superior force of the United   Minister
Plenipotentiary, His Excellency John L. Stevens, has caused United States troops to be landed at H   that he wo
uld support the said Provisional Government. Now, to avoid any collision of armed forces, and perhaps   do, unde
r this protest and impelled by said forces, yield my authority until such time as the Government of the   l, upon
the facts being presented to it, undo (?) the action of its representative, and reinstate me in the autho   as the
constitutional sovereign of the Hawaiian Islands. Done at Hono   s seventeenth day of January   D.   he
re was any danger?" I answered, "There might be." The morning of   h of January, 1893, arrived w   the
closing of the legislature. At 10 A.M. I called a cabinet meeting   purpose of apprising them of th   Hou
se, and other preliminary instructions. I told them it was my in   promulgate a new constitution. The   et
the legislature, and we adjourned. At 12 M. I prorogued the legi   noticed that the   was not fill   g.
There were many ladies present in the audience, and I also no   everal members of   atu   on   efor
m party were not there. This looked ominous of some coming trouble   ring the palace   ch
e Blue Room. I went up to him, and asked if it was all ready   Then   id. "Y   day:"
and I pa   ed into the Blue Room, and sat awaiting my ministe   nger d
elay they arrived. I immediately judged from their countenan   I w
ould sign the constitution in the throne-room and in the pre   had been
elected by the people for the purpose of working for a new   nt fro
m all parts of the kingdom asking for a new constitution. Mr   aihee,
amauoha of Kohala, and other members came to me repeated   nncement
his ministry, advocated a new constitution, as well   to M
Parke   I had always said it would be a good thing, and he   d. A month
ter I   t two members of the legislature, and started to make up a   constitu   887. After
    ing it, I kept it until the month of October, when I   ced it i   hands o   corter
d heard of it already from Mr. Peterson. It appears that immediately on th   of my intentions, Mr. Cadburn,   the morni
ng of the 14th of January, immediately acted the part of a traitor, by going to Mr. Hartwell, a lawyer, and informing him of my in
tentions, and of course received instructions from him to strongly advise me to abandon the idea. This, then, was the cause of th
e delay and my long waiting in the Blue Room. The members of the diplomatic corps had been invited, also the members of the min
e bench and members of the legislature, besides a committee of t   Kalak na. The latter were invited to be present because it
was through them that many petitions had been sent to me. When th   I told them everything in the throne-room wa
s ready, and the guests were awaiting our presence; that we must not keep   I was surprised when the cabinet informed
me that they did not think it advisable for me to take such a step. th   of an uprising, etc. I told them   would
not have taken such a step if they had not encouraged me. They had   ge of a precipice, and now were le   ing me
to take the step alone. It was humiliating. I said, "Why not give the p   tion, and I will bear the brun   all t
he blame afterwards." Mr. Peterson said, "We have not read the c   had had it in his possess   hole m
onth. The three ministers left Mr. Parker to try to dissuad   eantime they all (Peterson   well
, and Colburn) went to the government building to inform Thurston   took. Of course they wer   structed
not to yield. When they went over everything was peaceful and quiet   ting patiently in the th   The min
isters returned, and I asked them to read the constitution over. At the end I asked them what they saw injurious   ocument.
Mr. Peterson said there were some points which he thought were not exactly suited. He begged that I should wait   eks; in
the meantime they would be ready to present it to me. With these assurances I yielded, and we adjourned to the th   oom. I sta
te to the guests present my reasons for inviting their presence. It was to promulgate a new constitution at the requ   t of my peop
le; that the constitution of 1887 was imperfect and full of defects. Turning to the chief justice, I asked,   so, Mr. Jud
d?" and he answered in the affirmative, in the presence of all the members assembled. I then informed the peopl   sembled that u
nder the advice of my ministers I had yielded, as they had promised that on some future day I could give the   new constitution.
I then asked them to return to their homes and keep the peace. Everything seemed quiet until Monday morning. Even if any great com
It was the disappointment in my ministry. At about ten A.M., Monday, the 16th of January, notice

SO HEART SOLDIERS MUST INSTEAD

BECOME was issued by my ministers, stating "that the position I took and the attempt

I made to promulga   new constitution was at *YOUR PALACE. THUS*

MY CRATERS
ORDER: TAKE THE BOY. LEAVE.

Leave. ——for

Nā pua rose o Maunawili   *The sweet rose of Maunawili*
I laila hia'ia nā manu   *'tis there the birds of love dwell*
Miki'ala i ka nani o ka liko   *and sip the honey from your lips——*

Leave.

                                          She leaves.

Yet despite the queen's warning

We are still ignorant—unsatisfied—lingering——

——failing to notice
how easily we erased
a monarch—all monarchs——

in favor of

    deskclerkmaidbartenderwaiterwaitressprostitutemasseuse

           tens of thousands   hotel rooms
                                  atop
                                  burial grounds
                                  fishing shrines
                                  ceremonial platforms
                                  ancient temples
         half all species   endangered

    deskclerkmaidbartenderwaiterwaitressprostitutemasseuse

drilling into Pele——

          deeper   deeper——

we can't stop——

fontanels not yet firm,

we climb through sulfurous clouds   gagging   to toss

          dimes/fish/piglets/Cheetos
          then kukui/plumeria/polyester roses

here goes a lamb
followed by

Tupperware glass
baking dishes/tires/
scrap metal/GMO wheat/disposable diapers

and finally Dell/selfie drones/
i- i- iphones

into Kīlauea crater
as our inflationary
fingers grasp for

MORE

glass coins of the realm————

How many Kentucky mountaintops
to blast?
How many crude-slick terns
to die among the mangroves?

    Oi, Neil, our conquest flag is metal >
so it never waves on the windless moon————

————to distract, Queen Liliʻuokalani sends us

  to our Cuban Googolplex
  Goddess of the Florida Keys,

  who sleeps spooning with us
  all night ~ all day

in our crystal conch bed domed palace
      of sand dollars and junonia

trans lucent semen   milk-tight
    coconut breasts

no bitbridles to our ecstasy

the joy of morning the hue~born nudibranch
      between her lips

She gives   ^ pomegranates ^ pawpaw
robes of vanilla

        sea cows pas de deux
      a choir of upside-down jellyfish
    the ∞ cornucopia   of imagined reality

Do you hear
(she asks on the leaving wind)
(her uterine discernment, by necessity,
lightless and deep)

all waters, amniotic, expressing their desire——
    > How can we reproduce ourselves? <

Like this!:
    The open set ~
    O ring within ring within ring O.

    ∞

    Soft Sheaves Fine Sheaves Flabby Sheaves
    ∞
    Tao Tau lotus unwinds
    ∞

So stop now————————————————————<
with me and own all that rises

from within and beyond this country,
within and beyond the mind:

the awakened one
earthairfirewater
*up*down*bottom*top*strange*charm*

The Three Jewels
    of Buddha * Dharma* * *Sangha*
creating evermore,

the wet~elastic scattering————

    ————of matter which tends
    toward increasing   complexity————

Look for me then
not *beneath* your bootsoles

but *on* your/their soles ~ *in* your/their soles
and *in* the silicon étale of all flesh

and *in* your soul always alone
always ahead < back turned

looking forward
on the tree-lined ∞ lane—

With each thought we make this world . . . .
. . . . like the fired glass melt~meld . . . .
. . . . of sand+soda ash+lime . . . .

Every sacred fig bud a small swelling . . . . every root softened with hairs . . . .
Every Bodhi tree, if slashed, growing upward leaving the wound . . . . healed
. . . . the same distance from the ground . . . .

There are no entirely black flowers . . . . only parts . . . .

I have heard the naysayers, the Occams . . . .

yet we shall multiverse . . . . talk only . . . .
of transworld identity . . . . wavefunction . . . .
all that is created and not created . . . .
the Ultimate Ensemble . . . .

Trespass/Étale
Past *dukkha* stressmiseryfrustrationdiscomfortpainsorrowafflictionsufferingunease

Neither beginnings nor endings nor accidents
the mandala of ancient parallel to youth

each failure pulling forward the spirit <

While we struggle to erase
America's perennial

HolyUnholyHolyUnholyHolyUnholyHoly
VirginWhoreVirginWhoreVirginWhore
GoddessBitchGoddessBitchGoddessBitch

Goddess————

————Listen Up, Allen, Take a Look
Under the Clitoral Hood:

The cosmos is holy! The spirit is holy! The uterus is holy! The endometrium is
holy! The cervix and clitoris and lips and fingers and hymen and anus holy!

Holy all mothers freed from insane asylums! Holy the cunts of the grandmothers
of Kansas! Holy the vulval! Holy the labium majora and minora! Holy the mons
veneris veneris veneris!

Holy the Bartholin's Glands!
Holy the Gräfenberg Spot!
Holy the Skene's Glands!

Holy the glass glory hole
and its glories!

O   O   O

Holy the ovaries!

Holy the fimbriae!

Holy the fallopian!

Holy the placenta!

Holy the amniotic!

Holy the umbilicus!

Holy the dilation!

Holy the midwives
and doulas and dowsers and diviners!

Holy the mucus plug, the bloody bloody bloody show!

————I write this to bait   *Any* Founders

Any Creators————

————with a tease:

Reveal all? I ask them. *Please?*

Uh-huh. See, we gave that last chick immortality
just as she requested—

but she found
it un-sat-is-fact-ory. With each complaint

a chunk
of her flesh fell off
until there was nothing but whine—

so we locked the sound
in a far closet
among the silk scarves fallen

like foamed sea. So why would *you*
be different than that she-beast?

Reveal all? I beg again. *Please?*
Rah-rah. If you're feeling a bit tub a bit soft
or, well, a bit not right

just jack out-up your hair: a big do
makes everything OK if mixed

with fierce-ass shoes. In battles you must
carry Hermès, not
be carried *by* Hermes—

refuse
to be made bride
or bleed——

——yet then the gods conjure

Sappho for my evening diversion.
Six gins, lingering—the rank Labrador
still outside, door scratch, forgotten *chick-*
chick-chickadee to bring the flock in. I bring
a husband's moon ears to slip spot, bubble
pop. The back and the burn. Spermatoblast,
so these

are the wasp hearts! Years and tears melted into one eager shine surge, star-flowered hearse. The else and its dark hooks recede, skies roll into bales. And yet: *Get off me,* I suddenly say, today's paper cut scissoring

a thumb as husband holds me fast. Still he remains: obtuse, granite. He whispers, *Happened to notice you've gained* (aprons and shrouds). *Really? Well, so have you. Not funny. Damn it—get off. Off!* Soon he lets the dog in, a new love stout and mucky with clawed

garden. I turn on my side, fuming. *Everyone dies,* I say. Dirges burn unheard in the distance, like torched dry mountain herbs. *What the heck? Where'd that come from?* Within me, a new soul has just begun,

drunk with pip. Its mouth full of driftwood, cottages and caverns: in nine months, a flaxen child. *Your turn to clean his paws*

that child says—
before it can speak—
before it is whole————

————knowing

of a burgeoning where, fingering night hills, you'll be far where folded, slobber rose soprano—but cannot fill alone.

So take fast your lover's hand, pull dream splay cracking into breasts—grass—castanets! And then, like a glimpse,

you will now mix
with us

into green glass. Broken———and Blended———

———and Knowing

we cannot be solely the inner cup,
always able to contain, or only the exterior lance———

or only———

~~ clown fish that sleep inside deadly sea anemones,
scarlet macaws that thrive on fatal fruit ~~

~~ stoats pregnant before they are weaned,
tsetse flies lactating for their young ~~

~~ the male sea horse brooding eggs in his pouch,
a frog father growing tadpoles within vocal sacs ~~

~~ the hermaphrodite barnacle rejecting itself as a mate,
wrasse fish that begin life as females, end as males———

———so at last prescribes our paraquadri,
                                        our suet, our soothe:

Our plants will
grow healthier

if newborn ~
adored,

if exalted
and stroked.
                    Then sends winds
                    Through our fingers.

All chairwheels and burnish
and ringrolls and merge.

                    Her/His Pure Land
                    round and round
                    rivers within stone———

O come again, s/he calls out———

O come now——

to our

     Apache/huisache   Sahnish/saskatoon—

     grama+galleta+sprangletop+bluestem+seaoats+tridens—
     gaura+gayfeather+lemonmint+phlox+prairiedawn—
     rushpea+dogweed+starcactus+bladderpod+chaffseed—
     rivershiner+pupfish+chubsucker+gambusia+blindcat—
     sheepfrog+ridley+hornedlizard+Texassiren+lyresnake—
     whoopingcrane+woodstork+prairiechicken+curlew—
     meshweaver+harvestman+amphipod+rifflebeetle—
     pimpleback+fawnsfoot+pigtoe+goldenorb+fatmucket—
     redwolf+ocelot+jaguarundi+manatee+humpback—
     Kamaʻo+Kauaʻi Oʻo+ʻAkialoa+Nukupuʻu+Poʻouli—

                > *OHELO ʻAI!* <

Yes, our *America—wildborn anew*—

yuccaplant=yuccamoth   cattleegret=bull
clownfish=anemone   gobyfish=shrimp
plover=crocodile   dairyingant=aphid
woman=l.reuteri   riverbankgrape=mite

no
zebramusselkudzunutriasnakeheadhydrillagypsymoth

only
lichen*lichen*lichen*lichen* lichen*lichen*lichen*lichen*
lichen*lichen*lichen*lichen* lichen*lichen*lichen*lichen*——<

       ——Hear mice sing blues with lichen in the dusk
       meadows? says the child. They know *all* pulled to shore
       collected stored eaten is less. Yet humming warm milk
       begins to hem in snow geese. Butterflies become graylight
       scatters on the cabbage rose chair.

       Now comes Mother and thick candles talking. Brined,
       her deep sea lights of story swing from finned honeybees.
       Beyond window, boat flowers on willow pond, dream

boughs like sleep. At last black nightsky and its forever
desire, *our* forever desire: *Shell.*

Rows of fangs and their spares now have no choice but to
be caught. Doubtless water sounding in the dark is just
rain! And this day? Ding-gone—a hive of velvet spires.
Fleecy ships, thorns of down, finally the *All* soft——<

because pain
has been long sung   *enough.*   Brake. Behold!

It's just that my river nectar
requires the right
love. The fat

orchards arrive
from distance   and recover my plumed

villages. I'm a new owner—
of a smug sunset

over fields
of blossom. Here, pull

my caravan
mystery thread. Then
dames and gents

begin to dance
for this——for me——for us——for our sails.

<
Ah, that *yes!* is our hats again
mooring.   Gulf, *Gulf!*

Yield in us
to a bay——

——where pistol shrimp
bubbles can reach
the temperature of our sun—

anemones nudge
our warm breasts
into plush mouths
and then suck—

an octopus mates by inserting
a sperm packet
into the head
of its lover—

frilling shark's wound affirms:
this crimson is
our horticulture—

> the waving seaweed
> at last crowns
> itself and becomes
> *The* Book——

——so if you enter me
from behind—marry
the seas with my rings within rings—

all fins all feet waking—
not walking—as buckeye
blossoms and bristlegrass

watch, you unfold me plumb—

yes, you unfold me plumb—O O O—

to be pinned by sand
stone and its vacant

mineral *yum*—the self-
righteous,
upright wheat

leaf taking, leave taking—at last
standing bent-broken
in the sheaf-less

hearts of the gods.

~

If I enter you
from behind, we will hunch

wet beneath New
Mexico cave

coral as our pelts heat
to glass—and watch

the buffalo peel
back her skin, revealing

a woman melting but bloom-
fine—

~

To mate is to bind.

Foolishly fearing
that merge, we can't help shooting

arrow after arrow, bullet
after bullet into the enormous

grizzly. Placid—bloodless—the bear
finally pulls them out, polishes

each on silvertip coat,

and then hurls them back at us. Grinning.

~

At that moment in 1776 we died————————————————

~

————————So what of the dead's blood what of the dead?

How mystic how maternity   our water

yes our water   swims centuries,   no halt
            to the flowing   wheeling worlds————

——because tornadoes, although whirling, contain cores

of peace

surrounding   ringing

the Cherokee trapper—scalped, punched
    through with buckshot, abandoned for dead—
binding her head, praying
    through bloodhole gums, crawling
two miles to her nearest neighbor—   *She is you*

and the pale, freckled fiddler at the Little Rock
    hoedown, whipsawing his bow
    from atop the burl oak
where he was hoisted, rope knotted
    to a saddle—for protection
    against wayward slaps, bullet sprays—
until he falls, accidentally hangs to death,
    while everyone fails to notice, dancing—   *He is you*

and the black rancher pitting
    hands, twisting fingers
    while stripping thorns from prickly pear
cattle feed during the drought
    that has made his ranch a desert,
never a home—   *He is you*

and the prostitute celebrating her birthday
    at the beach track, mini cars on dunes, dust puffs, din
    like storms of hornets—*What do you want,*
honey? the owner says, showing
    a motorcycle and a jeep, *One rut or two?*—
Dos! she replies, smiling, figuring
    she could control a two-wheeler better, then drinks
beer and races for hours, blood rivulets
    lacing scrapes on hands, elbows, knees   *She is you*

and the plane passengers
standing nipple-high
in the iced Hudson, waiting
for police barges/ferries/tugboats   *They are you*

and the Japanese-American soldier—one arm in pieces
but detached hand still holding a grenade—prying
pineapple from dead fingers and tossing it at the Gothic
Line as he hollers obscene limericks   *He is you*

and the 80 percent of North Dakota "wild"
canola, painting roadsides electric citron,
harboring Roundup Ready genes
in its four-leaf clover flowers   *It is you*

and the deathpale Wyoming college boy, gay,
robbedtorturedtied to a fence until
a passing cyclist mistakes him for a scarecrow,
stops to look closer, runs for help   *He is you*

and the first-grade teacher
PuertoRicanIrishAmerican
charging like a bull and dying
as a shield to protect students from the shooter   *She is you*

and the corpse of a Laysan albatross
chick, stuffed like a piñata with shredded
plastic garbage bags, bottle caps, and nets
collected by its mother who thought they were squid   *He is you*

and the Eyak painter
daubing needlepoint designs
of abstract, fractal cities
for her autistic son to stroke and stitch   *She is you*

and the World War I Doughboy
trembling naked in the snow
while his clothes are steamed
for liceticksfleas   *He is you*

and the dental office secretary, *kānaka maoli,*
who is trans* and lives
in a geodesic dome to save paychecks
for hormones and surgery   *She is you*

and the frantic earthworms awash
in endosulfan–aldicarb–carbaryl,
unable to form sperm, no amber
egg pearls in the compost   *They are you*

and the Samoan grandmother wading
from the Ninth Ward
in a flowered coral raincoat,
Ziplocs of panties tied to raised wrists   *She is you*

and the black scientist
conquering the boll weevil
by inventing paintplasticgasolinenitroglycerin
from peanuts   *He is you*

and the Bohemian Waxwing flock,
cockeyed pirates, rattle-trilling with fury
because the crab apple trees, too hot
too soon, failed to set fruit   *They are you*

and the first Asian-American Marine Corps Officer
shouting in Chinese, *Don't shoot! I'm Chinese!*
as he runs forward in sacrifice, protecting his battalion
against Chinese troops in the Korean War   *He is you*

and the shirtless, rib-knob-thin homeless trumpeter,
psychotic, skin deep copper,
using metal pipe blowguns and pebble
bullets to kill city pigeons for food   *He is you*

and the six-foot Haitian-American actress
stretching cervical mucus between thumb
and forefinger, clutching her wife's hand,
plunging in a sperm syringe   *She is you*

and the first calves born to orcas, dying
due to breastmilk pollutants accrued for years, their
brief toxin-sponge lives allowing second calves
to fare better and sometimes live   *They are you*

and the Belizean sculptor
forging chandelier dream catchers from
brokenglass/cigarettebutts/shotgunshells/cocainebags
left in Bronx lots   *He is you*

and the Houston widow,
her firefighter husband
killed in a chicken farm blaze, no inheritance because
she once changed her sex   *She is you*

and the coppery male Potomac River
smallmouth bass, glisten-green plump,
immature female eggs studding
its sex organs   *He is you*

and the gentle Jasper father lynch-dragged conscious,
miles in chains, body found in 81 different places,
decapitated, grave desecrated twice,
racial slurs, profanities, headstone overturned   *He is you*

and the former Baptist Preacher, now a b-boy,
traveling from city hall to city hall, spinning and suiciding
and spouting to publicize the Great Pacific
Garbage Patch gyre with his feet and furious words   *He is you*

and the thirteen-year-old boy in a hoodie, dangling
a toy airsoft AK-47, shot seven times
by a terrified cop, an Iraq war veteran who
handcuffs him before performing CPR   *He is you*

and the female pica whistling
all day in hope of finding a mate or even just
another, but the once cold mountains have warmed them
all into death, thistles without seed, shriveled berries   *She is you*

and the double amputee winning bronze
in Paralympics snowboarding, three days later
dazzling in a swooping-swiveling cha-cha,
15 years after she was given a 2% chance at life   *She is you*

and the starving Lakota POW
in Vietnam, rare rations of pig food and cabbage,
shoulders dislocated from suspension by ropes, tapping
secret code messages on walls to sustain others   *He is you*

and the belugas so infused
with herbicides, pesticides, and phosphorus
that they have intestinal cancer, and it is law
that their carcasses are handled as toxic waste   *They are you*

and the 22-year-old cancer survivor, pregnant,
having her breasts amputated
because the implants leak vegetable oil, bacteria
migrating to her spasming fetus   *She is you*

and the Geomagic founder, forced into factory work
at age eight in China, communist child soldier,
landing in America at 25 with only $80, years
later a millionaire dancing at Burning Man,
silver mask, violet streaks ribboning her hair   *She is you*

and the woman screaming, biting the rapist
who grabs her from behind, drags her into the elevator,
saying "I just want to love you, baby"—she gouges
his eyes, nose, kicks the emergency intercom
button until, sobbing, moaning, he runs   *She is you*

and the redback salamander, jasper stripe
aglow, unable to lay her eggs at night
due to security beacons glaring
from suburban tract homes   *She is you*

and the Guatemalan vitamin bottler, hair aflame,
uniform aflame after she mistakenly cleaned a machine
with alcohol—soon trying to leap from the Pittsburgh
ambulance, terrified of doctors because she has no papers   *She is you*

. . .

and the one-eyed, bald Vermont palm reader who says,
Your life will be embroidered with milky galaxies
of children, then lifts his head, turns up palms,
opens like a heart to sacrament   *He is you*

and the Jewish great-aunt, tucking a Salt Lake afghan
around her Mormon niece, describing swimming
through a winter lake, fleeing Germany for Switzerland,
searchlights, gun cracks that took
her mother, father, brothers   *She is you*

and the Nazi soldier, decades later in Idaho, who can't
stop remembering how he relaxed at base after hunting
them—Riesling and sauerbraten, Biedermeier,
beeswax candles—cozy fire, yet cold rain so driving,
so unforgiving he cannot open the door after to go home   *He is you*

and the American drone kill-shredding
a Pakistani midwife grandmother, *the string that held*
our family together, as she gathers okra
with grandchildren also cut and burned   *It is you*

and the Thai father crying silently as he cooks for hours,
making comfort food for his daughter raped at Fort Dix—
pak bung fai daeng (stir-fried morning glories),
yam pla duk fu (fried catfish with green mango salad),
phat kaphrao (prawns sautéed with Thai holy basil),
chao kuai (grass jelly with brown sugar, shaved ice)   *He is you*

and the wild blueberry bushes,
their tiny blush pantaloons
blooming six weeks earlier
than when Thoreau wrote *Walden*   *They are you*

and the mere seven orchid species
that remain, brown-bent and curling,
from the twenty-one he catalogued
in journals   *They are you*

and the mountain mint blossoms
he forded like bridal veil froth
among the woods and fields
but cannot be found now   *They are you*

and the Smoky Mountains synchronous
fireflies flashing in waves
or greatbursts followed always—
always—by pauses of darkness—   *They are you*——

——and in that darkness,
our healer and annealer,

a nuptial chamber
of nirvana

(united and untied)
beckons—

and questions—

So the gods, streaming,
take up bellows to answer,

to birth our new
molten country. Within

their forming glass bubble, we
soften and meld, each

a pitcher of opera without grief
or shame

as the orb hardens
around our rill. Elastic,

ecstatic, the rushes
enter

and keep. O darling,
O calendar of charm,

Your gaze a willow and lips
of ribbon,

royal rings—to burn
holds every form:

no *more*, no *how*:

                              Gone is the supervision
                              of dust.

THANKS

I was privileged to have Marjorie Perloff transform my understanding of the 1855 first edition of *Leaves of Grass*. I am indebted to Marjorie for igniting my passion for poetry and for planting the seed of this book.

The idea of glass sheaves was triggered by Jacqueline Berting's visionary *The Glass Wheatfield*, an installation of fourteen thousand waist-high, transparent, individually crafted glass stalks of wheat. The three glass wheat stalks in the frontispiece photograph were sculpted by Ms. Berting.

I first began writing this poem after Paul Slovak inadvertently inspired me to study Buddhism. I am thankful to him for introducing me to the Buddhist principles threaded throughout this work. Without a Buddhist perspective, I would have been unable even to begin writing the poem. I am also grateful for his kindness, wise editorial advice, and patience.

Allusions to the Sixth Extinction were informed by T. C. Boyle's novel *A Friend of the Earth* ("Because to be a friend of the Earth, you have to be an enemy of the people"). I am also grateful to Tom for being such a generous mentor to me when I was a young writer.

In addition, I was influenced a great deal by Elizabeth Kolbert's *The Sixth Extinction: An Unnatural History*, *Silent Spring* by Rachel Carson, Naomi Klein's *This Changes Everything: Capitalism vs. the Climate*, Philippe Squarzoni's *Climate Changed*, and many works by Bill McKibben. The films of Josh Fox and the movies *Plastic Planet* and *Plastic Paradise* also altered my thinking. (The references to albatrosses in the poem are rooted in *Plastic Paradise* as well as in *The Rime of the Ancient Mariner*. I encourage readers to view photographs of dead, plastic-filled albatross chicks online.)

There are references and feminist riffs in the poem responding to and rebutting aspects of "seminal" texts about the American experience. Those texts include, among others, Carl Sandburg's *The People, Yes*, Hart Crane's *The Bridge*, Allen Ginsberg's *Howl*, Herman Melville's *Clarel*, Vladimir Nabokov's *Pale Fire*, W. S. Merwin's *The Folding Cliffs*, Ezra Pound's *Cantos*, John Dos Passos's trilogy *U.S.A.*, and William Carlos Williams's *Paterson* . . . and of course Walt Whitman's *Leaves of Grass*.

I am thankful for Pi'ilani Ko'olau's memoir *Kaluaikoolau!*, which was critical for the Hawai'i section of the poem. Frances N. Frazier's translation of that memoir, *The True Story of Kaluaikoolau*, was essential to my understanding of the place and period. As mentioned in the Preface, the text used to create the fading images of Queen Lili'uokalani is from her heartbreaking memoir *Hawai'i's Story by Hawai'i's Queen*.

Other books I consulted included Zitkala-Ša's *American Indian Stories, Impressions of an Indian Childhood*, and *Dreams and Thunder: Stories, Poems, and the Sun Dance Opera*. Roseanne Hoefel's *Zitkala-Ša: A Biography* was very helpful. I referred many times to Ida B. Wells's *Southern Horrors: Lynch Law in All Its Phases, The Light of Truth: Writings of an Anti-Lynching Crusader*, and *Crusade for Justice: The Autobiography of Ida B. Wells*. The two italicized quotations in the "Ida of Wells, Wells of Ida" section are her words. Charlotte Perkins Gilman's *The Living of Charlotte Perkins Gilman, Herland*, and *Women and Economics* were influential, as was Cynthia Davis's *Charlotte Perkins Gilman: A Biography*. For the poem's references to Lucy Gonzalez Parsons, I am indebted to Carolyn Ashbaugh for her *Lucy Parsons: American Revolutionary*, and of course to Gonzalez Parsons herself for *Freedom, Equality & Solidarity: Writings & Speeches, 1878–1937* (Revolutionary Classics). The timeless italicized phrases in the "Lucy and the Parsons of Anarchy" section are all hers.

Aimé Césaire's anticolonial poetics influenced every word of this book. ("I have a different idea of a universal. It is a universal rich with all that is particular, rich with all the particulars there are, the deepening of each particular, the coexistence of them all." —Aimé Césaire)

The extraordinary poets Dean Young and Tomaž Šalamun read this poem in its early form and gave me invaluable advice.

Matt Richardson and his scholarship were a beacon.

David Lehman's lovely book *The Daily Mirror: A Journal in Poetry* was the impetus behind some of "Inception."

Parts of the poem's conclusion were originally written as an epithalamion for the incandescent Mimi Chubb.

I was able to cope with the many miscarriages addressed in this poem thanks to Elizabeth McCracken's remarkable *An Exact Replica of a Figment of My Imagination*. Her story always made me feel comforted and less alone. Thank you, Elizabeth.

. . .

Thank you to the magazines and books where parts of the poem *Plenty* were first published, in different form.

Six excerpts were included in *Best American Poetry*.

One section, published in *Illuminations*, was nominated for a Pushcart Prize.

Several lengthy excerpts were published in *Drunken Boat* as a Bernadette Mayer Folio.

Two chapbook-length passages were published in *Verse* and later included in *The Best of Verse* anthology.

Other fragments were published in *Beloit Poetry Journal*, *Counterexample*, *Feature Magazine*, *Many Mountains Moving*, *New Verse*, *Poecology*, *Posit*, *Red Booth Review*, *Short Fiction Collective*, and *Superflux*.

. . .

I am grateful to Kathleen Peirce, Hannah Chapelle Wojciehowski, Rod Flagler, Robert Wilson, Elizabeth Cullingford, Michael Adams, Laura Cottam-Sajbel, Angela Black, Kurt Heinzelman, Oscar Casares, I-Pei Hsiu-Hodge, Judith Kroll, Peter LaSalle, Gretchen Murphy, Lisa Moore, Elizabeth Richmond-Garza, Mary Ruefle, Laurie Saurborn, Carrie Fountain, Pattiann Rogers, Aileen Hays, and my children for their encouragement and their example.

The writing of this poem was supported by much-needed funds from the estates of James A. Michener and E. L. Keene. Thank you. John Crawley's summer writing grant via the New Writers Project was especially helpful, an unexpected and necessary boon. I am thankful for his generous support.

Boundless gratitude to Eric Chapelle for the lovely music and soundscapes he created for a partial recording of this poem.

Colin Doyle created the frontispiece to this book, as well as many images associated with parts of the poem online and in print. I am thankful beyond measure for his beautiful work.

• • •

Frontispiece:
"Glass Sheaf." (Glass wheat created by Jacqueline Berting.) Photograph by Colin Doyle. Used by permission of the photographer.

A kind in glass and a cousin, a spectacle and nothing strange a single hurt color and an arrangement in a system to pointing. All this and not ordinary, not unordered in not resembling. The difference is spreading.

—GERTRUDE STEIN, Tender Buttons

Tikkun Olam

סלוע ןוקית

Repair the World

Laura Kay Wootan

ABOUT THE AUTHOR

Corinne Lee's poetry, fiction, and nonfiction have been published in dozens of literary magazines. Her debut collection, *PYX*, was selected by Pattiann Rogers as a winner of the National Poetry Series competition and was published by Penguin. Lee was educated at the University of Southern California, the Iowa Writers' Workshop, and the University of Texas at Austin. A master naturalist and an environmentalist who specializes in water quality issues, she lives in the Texas Hill Country.

PENGUIN POETS